GW00703238

MALAYSIAN FAVOURITES

Lee Mee Yoong
Yoong Sit Ying

Delta Publishing Sdn Bhd

Delta Publishing Sdn Bhd
(A Member of Delta Publishing Group of Companies)
Wisma Delta
18 Jalan 51A/223
46100 Petaling Jaya
Selangor Darul Ehsan
MALAYSIA
Tel: 603 – 7570000
Fax: 603 – 7576688/7587001
Telex: MA 20382 AB DELTA

© Delta Publishing Sdn Bhd

*All rights reserved. No part of this publication may be
reproduced, stored in a retrieval system, or transmitted,
in any form or by any means, electronic, mechanical,
photocopying, recording or otherwise, without the prior
permission of the publisher.*

First Edition 1993
Second Edition 1995

Perpustakaan Negara Malaysia   Cataloguing-in-Publication Data

Lee, Mee Yoong
    Malaysian Favourites/
    Lee Mee Yoong, Yoong Sit Ying
    ISBN 983-9808-03-6
    1. Cookery--Malaysia. 2. Cookery, Malaysian.
    I. Yoong, Sit Ying. II. Title
    641.59595

Printed in Malaysia by **Baron Production Sdn Bhd**

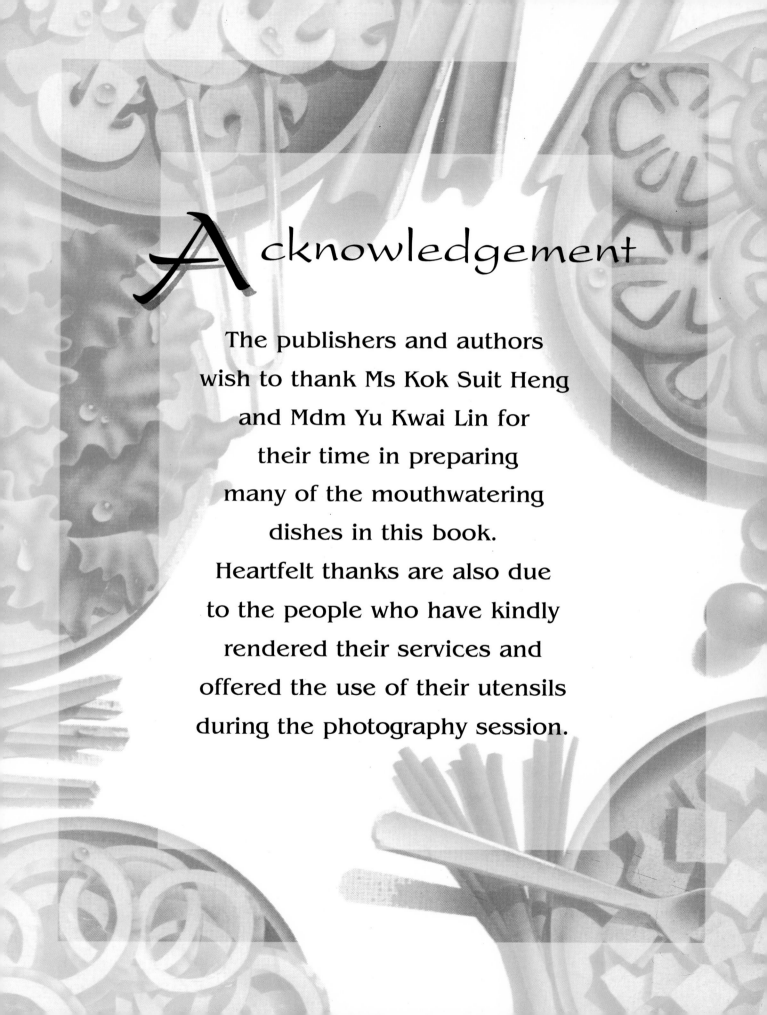

Acknowledgement

The publishers and authors
wish to thank Ms Kok Suit Heng
and Mdm Yu Kwai Lin for
their time in preparing
many of the mouthwatering
dishes in this book.
Heartfelt thanks are also due
to the people who have kindly
rendered their services and
offered the use of their utensils
during the photography session.

Introduction

Makanlah! A visit to a Malaysian home for dinner begins with this warm welcome that is the hallmark of Malaysian hospitality. The host will most likely offer his guest some refreshing local drink as a prelude to enjoying a meal together.

At lunch or dinner, Malaysians generally enjoy a meal with a variety of dishes. In addition to the obligatory bowl or plate of rice, there will often be a soup of some kind, a curry, a steamed fish, a fried dish, a salad and one or more of the basic sauces. Served at the same time will most likely be some dessert, a drink or fresh fruit. On the other hand, a one-dish meal at lunch or dinner is also common and acceptable. A typical Malaysian breakfast or tea takes the form of a bewildering and tantalising variety of *kuih*, or local cakes. The choice is very wide.

Included in this book are the ever popular Malaysian favourite dishes which are, on the whole, simple and nutritious. Local readers who enjoy these dishes but may not know how to prepare them will find the dishes presented here actually simple and practical to prepare.

The ingredients as well as some selected dishes are presented in a bilingual format (English – Malay). This is for the convenience of foreign readers who are residing in or visiting the country. It is hoped that like the local readers they will also try their hand at preparing some delightful dishes the Malaysian way. The ingredients are readily available throughout Malaysia and the ASEAN region, even at Chinatown in most countries.

Jemputlah makan! Do help yourself!

The Publisher

CONTENTS

DRY INGREDIENTS
KEY:

1. Rice noodles/Meehoon
   (Mihun)

2. Dried sweet bean curd sheets
   (Timcuk)

3. Fennel
   (Jintan manis)

4. Candlenuts
   (Buah keras)

5. Lentils
   (Kacang dal)

6. Wheat flour vermicelli
   (Mi suah)

7. Dried chillies
   (Cili kering)

8. Black fungi/Mok yee

9. Dried shrimps
   (Udang kering)

10. Palm sugar
    (Gula melaka)

11. Cinnamon
    (Kayu manis)

12. Cardamom
    (Buah pelaga)

13. Black glutinous rice
    (Pulut hitam)

14. Garlic
    (Bawang putih)

15. Chick pea powder/Horse gram powder
    (Tepung kacang kuda)

16. Black fungi/Wan yee

17. Star anise
    (Bunga lawang)

18. Tamarind skins
    (Asam gelugur)

19. Mixed spice powder/Five-spice powder/Goh heong hun/Ng heong fun

20. Mustard seeds
    (Biji sawi)

21. Turmeric powder
    (Serbuk kunyit)

22. Mustard powder
    (Serbuk sawi)

23. Mungbean vermicelli/Sohoon

24. Cloves
    (Bunga cengkih)

25. White peppercorns
    (Lada putih)

26. Anchovies
    (Ikan bilis)

27. Fried bean curd balls/taw foo pok
    (Tauhu bulat goreng)

28. Shrimp paste
    (Belacan)

29. Dried bean curd skin
    (Fucuk)

ix

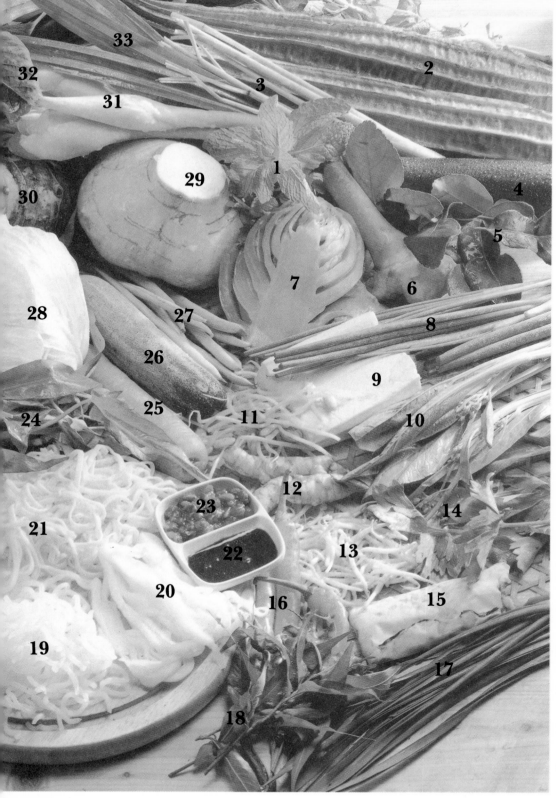

10. Chinese flowering cabbage/
    Mustard leaves (Sawi)

11. Large beansprouts
    (Tauge kasar)

12. Turmeric
    (Kunyit)

13. Beansprouts
    (Tauge)

14. Chinese celery
    (Daun saderi)

15. Fermented soya beans
    (Tempe)

16. Chillies
    (Cili)

17. Chinese chives
    (Kucai)

18. Annatto leaves
    (Daun kesum)

19. Laksa noodles
    (Mi laksa)

20. Flat rice noodles/Kway teow
    (Kuetiau)

21. Wheat noodles/Mee
    (Mi)

22. Prawn paste
    (Petis)

23. Soyabean paste
    (Taucu)

24. Water spinach
    (Kangkung)

25. Carrot
    (Lobak merah)

26. Cucumber
    (Timun)

27. French beans
    (Kacang buncis)

28. Head cabbage
    (Kubis)

29. Yam bean/Jicama
    (Sengkuang)

30. Yam/Taro
    (Keladi)

31. Ginger flower
    (Bunga kantan)

32. Chinese spinach
    (Bayam)

33. Screwpine leaves/*Pandan* leaves
    (Daun pandan)

WET INGREDIENTS
KEY:

1. Mint leaves
   (Daun pudina)

2. Angled luffa
   (Ketola sanding)

3. Lemon grass
   (Serai)

4. Brinjal/Egg-plant/
   Aubergine (Terung)

5. Lime leaves
   (Daun limau purut)

6. Galangal
   (Lengkuas)

7. Salted vegetables
   (Sayur masin)

8. Spring onions
   (Daun bawang)

9. Soft bean curd
   (Tauhu)

MEASURES, WEIGHTS, TEMPERATURES AND ABBREVIATIONS

Table Of Conversion

Imperial to Metric

Measures

1/8"	3 mm
1/4"	6 mm
1/2"	1½ cm
3/4"	2 cm
1"	2½ cm

Weight

½ ounces (oz)	15 g
1 oz	30 g
4 oz/¼ pound	120 g
8 oz/½ pound	240 g

Capacity

1/8 pints (pt)	70 ml
¼ pt	140 ml
½ pt	280 ml
¾ pt	420 ml
1 pt	560 ml
1¼ pt	700 ml
1½ pt	840 ml
1¾ pt	980 ml/⌒ 1 litre

Temperatures Of Stove Used

Explanation	Imperial	Metric	Gas
Cold	250°F – 270°F	120°C – 140°C	½ – 1
}	300°F – 325°F	150°C – 170°C	2 – 3
Medium Heat }	350°F – 375°F	180°C – 190°C	4 – 5
Hot	400°F – 425°F	200°C – 220°C	6 – 7
High Heat	450°F – 475°F	230°C – 240°C	8 – 9

Abbreviations

tbsp — tablespoon;   dsp — dessertspoon;   tsp — teaspoon.

GARNISHES

SPRING ONION **2**

FRIED SHALLOTS **2**

CHILLIES **2**

CUCUMBER **3**

CARROT **4**

LIME **4**

Garnishes

The aim for garnishing food is to add colour to the food to make it look more attractive. Garnishes must be arranged properly and there should not be too many. Spring onion, chillies, fried shallots, carrot, cucumber and lime are ingredients for garnishing food that can be eaten raw and are suitable for savoury dishes. Taste, smell and colour must be suitable for the food to be garnished.

Spring Onion

First Method

- Cut spring onion 5 cm/2" long. Make several slits 2 cm/¾" lengths along both ends with a pin or a sharp knife.
- Soak in water and leave in the refrigerator for the ends to curl.
- Use as desired.

Variation

* Cut chilli rings.
* Put spring onion strips into chilli rings before slitting the ends.

Second Method

- Spring onion can be diced 6 cm/¼" long to be sprinkled on food such as soup or porridge.

Fried Shallots

- Peel shallots and slice thinly crosswise.
- Heat oil in wok.
- Add in sliced shallots and fry till golden brown over low fire.
- Remove from oil. Cool.
- Keep in airtight container.
- Use as desired.

Chillies

First Method

Chilli curls
- Cut chilli lengthwise into two.
- Remove seeds.
- Shred chilli lengthwise.
- Soak in water and leave in the refrigerator for the chilli strips to curl.
- Use as desired.

Second Method

Chilli flowers
- Cut chilli from pointed end to a little before the stalk.

Garnishes

- Remove seeds.
- Cut again 2 or 3 times to get 6 - 8 sections which are joined together.
- Soak in water and leave in the refrigerator for the sections to curl.
- Use as desired.

Variation

* Cut away the pointed end and cut as below.

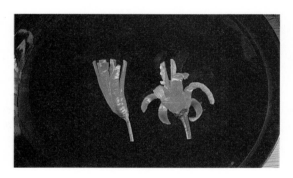

Cucumber

First Method

- Slice cucumber 3 mm/⅛ " thick.
- Cut as shown in photograph.

Second Method

- Cut cucumber 3¾ cm/1½" long.
- Shape as shown in photograph.
- Slice lengthwise 3 mm/⅛" thick.

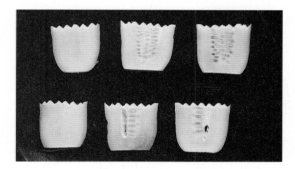

Third Method

- Slice cucumber rings 3 mm/⅛" thick.
- Slice as shown in photograph.
- Twist cucumber.

Variation

* Lime or lemon can be shaped as in third method above.

Garnishes

Carrot

First Method
- Slice carrot 3 mm/¼" thick.
- Shape carrot slices like butterflies or desired shapes.

Second Method
- Cut carrot 5 cm/2" long.
- Cut small wedges from sides 1½ cm/½" apart or distance as desired.
- Cut slices of 3 - 6 mm/⅛ - ¼" crosswise.

Variation
* Cucumber can be cut following second method.

Lime

First Method
- Slice lime 3 mm/⅛" thick.
- Shape lime slices like butterflies.

Second Method
- Cut wedges lengthwise to get 6 - 8 wedges.

SAUCES

INSTANT CHILLI SAUCE 6

CHILLI SAUCE 6

CHILLI TOMATO SAUCE 6

CHILLI GARLIC SAUCE 6

SWEET AND SOUR SAUCE 7

SALAD SAUCE 7

CHILLI SHRIMP PASTE SAUCE 9
(SAMBAL BELACAN)

SOYABEAN PASTE SAUCE 9
(SOS TAUCU)

BARBECUE SAUCE 9

COCONUT MILK SAUCE 10

CHOCOLATE SAUCE 10

CUSTARD SAUCE 10

SAUCES

Instant Chilli Sauce

This sauce is suitable for macaroni pie, fried rice noodles/fried meehoon, steamed yam cake, savoury pancake roll (*kuih dadar pedas*), dried shrimps in fried batter (*cucur udang/ cucur bawang*), fried meat balls, prawn fritters, fish balls and savoury steamed pudding (*kuih talam berlauk*).

> 1 tbsp tomato sauce
> 2 tbsp chilli sauce

- Mix the two sauces together, evenly.

Chilli Sauce

This sauce is suitable for macaroni pie, savoury steamed pudding (*kuih talam berlauk*), soft bean curd balls and fried vegetarian rice noodles/fried vegetarian meehoon.

> 3 red chillies
> 1 dsp vinegar
> 1 dsp fine sugar
> pinch of salt
> 1 dsp water
> } or to taste

- Pound chillies finely.
- Add in the other ingredients and mix well. Taste.

Chilli Tomato Sauce

This sauce is suitable for steamed yam cake, savoury pancake roll (*kuih dadar pedas*) and fried meat balls.

> 3 red chillies
> 1 dsp tomato sauce
> 1 tsp fine sugar
> 1 dsp vinegar
> pinch of salt
> 1 - 1½ dsp water
> } or to taste

- Pound chillies finely.
- Add in the other ingredients.
- Mix evenly. Taste.

Chilli Garlic Sauce

This sauce is suitable for stuffed hard bean curd (*taukua sumbat*), stuffed soft bean curd (*tauhu sumbat*), savoury fried tapioca fritters (*cucur ubi kayu*), vegetable puffs (*epok-epok sayur*), fried rice noodles/fried meehoon (*mihun goreng*) and fried vegetarian rice noodles/fried vegetarian meehoon.

> 3 red chillies
> 1 pip garlic
> 1 tbsp vinegar
> ¼ tsp salt
> 1 tsp fine sugar
> 1 - 1½ tbsp water
> } or to taste

- Pound chillies and garlic finely.
- Add in the other ingredients. Mix evenly. Taste.

SAUCES

Sweet and Sour Sauce

This sauce is suitable for fried fish, prawn fritters, fish balls, stuffed soft bean curd (*tauhu sumbat*) and fried meat balls.

2 tbsp tomato sauce
1 tbsp chilli sauce
1 dsp vinegar
1 dsp light soya sauce
1 tsp sugar } or to taste
⅛ tsp pepper
½ tsp cornflour
4 tbsp water
1 pip garlic
1 tbsp oil

- Chop garlic.
- Mix cornflour with 1 tbsp water.
- Heat oil. Fry garlic till golden brown.
- Add in all the other ingredients except cornflour mixture. Stir to mix evenly.
- When it bubbles, add in enough cornflour mixture to thicken.
- Simmer for a while. Taste.

Salad Sauce

This sauce is suitable for mixed vegetable salad, stuffed egg salad and prawn fritters.

1 tsp mustard powder (*serbuk biji sawi*)
1 tsp cornflour
3 dsp vinegar
1 tsp fine sugar
⅛ tsp salt
⅛ tsp pepper
1 tsp margarine
140 ml/¼ pt milk
1 hard-boiled egg – only yolk is used
a few drops of yellow colouring – optional

- Mix mustard powder with 1 dsp milk.
- Mix cornflour with 1 dsp milk.
- Add remaining milk, cornflour mixture, sugar, salt and pepper in a small saucepan.
- Stir till it simmers. Turn off fire.
- Add in mustard powder mixture.
- Mix evenly.
- Add in vinegar. Stir well.
- Add in margarine. Stir mixture over fire till it simmers and margarine has melted. Allow to cool.
- Stir in mashed egg yolk.
- If desired, yellow colouring can be added. Serve.

SAUCES

Chilli Shrimp Paste Sauce (Sambal Belacan)

This sauce is suitable for fried wheat noodles/ fried mee (*mi goreng*), fried rice noodles/ fried meehoon (*mihun goreng*), fried rice and coconut milk rice (*nasi lemak*).

6 red chillies
2 cm/¾" cube shrimp paste (*belacan*)
pinch of salt or to taste
½ tsp lime juice – optional

- Roast shrimp paste till crispy and with nice aroma.
- Pound it immediately with red chillies and salt.
- If desired, add lime juice before serving.

Soyabean Paste Sauce (Sos Taucu)

This sauce is suitable for egg and fish roll, stuffed soft bean curd (*tauhu sumbat*) and fried rice noodles Siamese style (*mi siam*).

1 tbsp soyabean paste (*taucu*)
1 pip garlic
1 tbsp oil
⅛ tsp pepper
1 tsp sugar or to taste
½ tsp cornflour
4 - 6 tbsp water
} mixed together

- Chop garlic and soyabean paste separately.
- Heat oil.
- Fry garlic till golden brown.

- Add in soyabean paste and fry for a while.
- Add in cornflour mixture and all the other ingredients.
- Simmer for a while. Taste.

Barbecue Sauce

This sauce is suitable for burger, fried meat balls, soft bean curd balls, macaroni pie, tomato salad and mixed vegetable salad.

1 dsp vinegar
½ tsp salt
1 tsp sugar
2 tbsp tomato sauce
1 tbsp chilli sauce
1 tsp mustard powder (*serbuk biji sawi*)
½ tsp thick soya sauce
1 tsp margarine
½ onion
140 ml/¼ pt water
2½ cm/1" cinnamon (*kayu manis*)
¼ star anise (*bunga lawang*)
10 white peppercorns (*lada putih*)

- Chop onion finely.
- Boil onion in water together with cinnamon, star anise and peppercorns until onion becomes soft and left with ½ the amount of water.
- Remove peppercorns, star anise and cinnamon.
- Add in vinegar, salt, sugar, tomato sauce, chilli sauce, thick soya sauce and margarine. Mix evenly.
- Simmer for three minutes. Taste.
- Add in mustard powder and mix well.

SAUCES

Coconut Milk Sauce

This sauce is suitable for pancake with grated coconut filling (*kuih ketayap*), agar (*agar-agar*) and stewed pineapple.

½ grated coconut to get 140 ml/¼ pt
coconut milk
¼ tsp salt
1 level tsp cornflour

- Add salt to coconut milk.
- Mix cornflour with 1½ dsp coconut milk.
- Heat remaining coconut milk and pour over cornflour mixture.
- Rinse saucepan.
- Heat coconut milk mixture till it thickens.
- Cool and serve as desired.

Chocolate Sauce

This sauce is suitable for steamed cake, agar (*agar-agar*) and ice-cream.

45 g/1½oz sugar
22 g/¾ oz brown sugar
22 g/¾ oz cocoa
140 ml/¼ pt milk
15 g/½ oz butter
¼ tsp vanilla essence

- Mix cocoa with 2 tbsp milk.
- Put all the ingredients in a rinsed saucepan and bring to boil, stirring all the time.

- When sugar has dissolved, simmer without stirring for three to five minutes over low fire.
- Serve hot or cold.

N.B. Preferably use a thick saucepan.

Custard Sauce

This sauce is suitable for steamed cakes, agar (*agar-agar*), fruit salad and stewed pineapple.

140 ml/¼ pt milk
1 tsp cornflour
1 dsp sugar or to taste
¼ tsp essence – type according to food to be served with
a few drops colouring

- Mix cornflour with 1 tbsp milk.
- Heat remaining milk with sugar in a rinsed saucepan.
- When sugar is dissolved, pour hot milk over cornflour mixture, stirring it as you pour.
- Rinse saucepan.
- Pour cornflour mixture, essence and colouring into saucepan.
- Stir to mix well. Lower fire.
- Simmer till it thickens.
- Serve sauce cold or hot.

PRESERVES

SALTED EGGS 12

PICKLED PAPAYA 12
(JERUK BETIK)

PICKLED CUCUMBER 13
(ACAR TIMUN)

PICKLED MIXED VEGETABLES 14
(ACAR RAMPAI)

PICKLED FISH 16
(ACAR IKAN)

PRESERVES

Salted Eggs

10 eggs
480 g/1 Ib salt
1 litre/1¾ pt water or enough water to
cover the eggs

- Boil water with salt. Cool.
- Wash eggs and put in a container (preferably earthen).
- Pour enough salt water to cover the eggs. Cover container.
- Leave eggs in salt water for two weeks before serving.

Pickled Papaya (Jeruk Betik)

300 g/10 oz raw papaya
2 red chillies
1 tsp salt
140 ml/¼ pt vinegar   } or to
2 tbsp sugar   taste

- Slice papaya thinly.
- Cut chillies lengthwise.
- Season papaya and chillies with salt for about half an hour.
- Rinse papaya and chillies. Wipe dry.
- Sun for half an hour.
- Mix vinegar and sugar until sugar dissolves. Taste.
- Add in papaya and chillies.
- Stand for about half a day before serving.

PRESERVES

Pickled Cucumber (Acar Timun)

1 medium-sized cucumber
8 shallots
2 red chillies
2 green chillies
1½ cm/½" ginger
1 stalk lemon grass (*serai*)
2 slices galangal (*lengkuas*)
2 pips garlic
1½ cm/½" turmeric (*kunyit*)
1 candlenut (*buah keras*)
4 tbsp vinegar ⎫
1 tbsp sugar ⎬ or to
¼ tsp salt ⎭ taste
2 tbsp oil

- Wash all vegetables and wipe dry.
- Cut cucumber six to eight wedges lengthwise.

- Cut away the centre. Cut again to 4 cm/ 1½" in length.
- Shred ginger.
- Cut chillies lengthwise.
- Sun cucumber, chillies, shallots and ginger for at least half an hour.
- Crush lemon grass.
- Pound galangal, garlic, turmeric and candlenut finely.
- Heat oil. Add in pounded ingredients. Fry pounded ingredients till there is nice aroma and oil appears.
- Add in lemon grass, vinegar, sugar and salt.
- Simmer for five minutes. Taste and cool.
- Add in vegetables and stand for at least half a day before serving.

Variation

* Carrot or yam bean/jicama (*sengkuang*) can also be used in place of cucumber.

PRESERVES

Pickled Mixed Vegetables
(Acar Rampai)

1 carrot
1 small cucumber
4 long beans
90 g/3 oz cauliflower
90 g/3 oz head cabbage (*kubis*)
2 red chillies
2 green chillies
10 dried chillies
2 stalks lemon grass (*serai*)
4 candlenuts (*buah keras*)
2 pips garlic
2½ cm/1" turmeric (*kunyit*)
2 cm/¾" galangal (*lengkuas*)
2 cm/¾" cube shrimp paste (*belacan*)
140 ml/¼ pt vinegar ⎫
2 tbsp sugar ⎬ or to
¼ tsp salt ⎪ taste
3 tbsp oil ⎭
2 tbsp peanuts

For Scalding Vegetables
3 tbsp vinegar
¼ tsp salt
280 ml/½ pt water

- Wash all vegetables and wipe dry.
- Cut carrot into six to eight wedges lengthwise.
- Cut carrot again into 4 cm/½" in length.
- Cut cucumber in the same manner as the carrot but cut away centre.
- Cut chillies lengthwise.
- Cut long beans, cauliflower and head cabbage.
- Boil 280 ml/½ pt water with 3 tbsp vinegar and ¼ tsp salt.
- Scald all the vegetables separately.
- Strain and dry in the sun for at least half an hour.
- Soak dried chillies in hot water.
- Fry peanuts without oil over low fire, stirring all the time. Fry till peanut skin can be removed easily. Remove skin and pound finely.
- Slice lemon grass and galangal.
- Pound finely dried chillies, turmeric, galangal, lemon grass, candlenuts, shallots, garlic and shrimp paste.
- Heat oil. Fry pounded ingredients over low fire till there is nice aroma and oil appears.
- Add vinegar, sugar and salt. Mix well.
- Simmer for three minutes. Taste. Turn off fire.
- Add in vegetables. Mix evenly.
- Keep pickle in a bowl for at least half a day.
- Sprinkle pounded peanuts on pickle before serving.

PRESERVES

Pickled Fish (Acar Ikan)

300 g/10 oz Spanish mackerals/
threadfins/mullets (*tenggiri/senangin/*
belanak)
¼ tsp turmeric powder (*serbuk kunyit*)
¼ tsp salt
2 shallots
2 pips garlic
1 red chilli
1 green chilli
2½ cm/1" ginger
2½ cm/1" turmeric (*kunyit*)
70 ml/⅛ pt vinegar ⎫
1 tbsp sugar ⎬ or to taste
¼ tsp salt ⎭
140 ml/¼ pt water
1 dsp sesame seeds
6 tbsp oil

- Wash all vegetables and wipe dry.
- Slice shallots, garlic and turmeric lengthwise. Shred ginger.
- Cut chillies lengthwise.
- Sun all vegetables for half an hour.
- Clean fish and wipe dry.
- Cut fish into pieces if desired.
- Season fish with turmeric powder and salt.
- Fry sesame seeds without oil over low fire till golden brown.
- Fry fish with 4 tbsp oil till golden brown.
- Heat 2 tbsp oil. Fry turmeric slices to get flavour and colour. Remove turmeric.
- Add in vinegar, salt, sugar and enough water.
- Simmer for about five minutes. Taste.
- Cool vinegar mixture.
- Add in fish and vegetables.
- Stand pickled fish for at least half a day.
- Sprinkle sesame seeds on fish before serving.

SOUPS

BASIC ANCHOVY STOCK **18**

BASIC BONE STOCK **18**

EGG & CORN SOUP **18**

CHINESE SPINACH SOUP **19**

MIXED VEGETABLE SOUP **19**

MUNGBEAN VERMICELLI SOUP WITH DRIED SHRIMPS AND EGG **20**

ANGLED LUFFA SOUP **20**

SALTED VEGETABLE SOUP WITH SOFT BEAN CURD **23**

CHICKEN SOUP **23**

CHICKEN AND VEGETABLE SOUP **23**

BEEF SOUP **24**

MUTTON SOUP **24**

SOUPS

Basic Anchovy Stock

1 rice bowl anchovies (*ikan bilis*)
3 - 4 pieces ginger
1 tbsp oil
840 ml/1½ pt water

- Wash anchovies. Shred ginger.
- Heat oil in pot. Fry ginger lightly.
- Add in anchovies and fry till golden brown.
- Add in water and simmer for 15 minutes. Use stock for soup.

N.B. Strain to remove anchovies or use the stock with anchovies in it.

Basic Bone Stock

300 g/10 oz bones
5 black peppercorns
1 litre/1¾ pt water

- Crush peppercorns.
- Put bones, crushed peppercorns and water in a pot.
- Bring to boil. Lower fire and simmer for about half an hour.
- Use stock with bones or remove bones from stock.

Egg and Corn Soup

For Stock
1 rice bowl anchovies (*ikan bilis*)
3 - 4 pieces ginger
1 tbsp oil
840 ml/1½ pt water

Other Ingredients
150 g/5 oz prawns
½ tin cream style corn
1 egg
1 tsp cornflour
salt & pepper to taste

- Chop prawns. Add in cornflour, salt and pepper. Mix evenly and shape into small balls.
- Beat egg.
- Prepare stock following method in recipe of Basic Anchovy Stock in this section.
- Add in prawn balls and boil for one minute.
- Add in cream style corn, stirring all the time.
- Lower fire. Add in egg, stirring all the time.
- Add salt to taste. Serve hot.

Variation
* You may use 90 g/3 oz minced meat in place of prawn balls.

SOUPS

Chinese Spinach Soup

For Stock

1 rice bowl anchovies (*ikan bilis*)
3 - 4 pieces ginger
1 tbsp oil
840 ml/1½ pt water
salt to taste

Other Ingredient

300 g/10 oz Chinese spinach (*bayam*)

- Prepare stock following method in recipe of Basic Anchovy Stock.
- Separate leaves from stems of Chinese spinach.
- Cut stems about 5 cm/2" long.
- Put Chinese spinach and stock in pot.
- When boiling, lower fire and simmer for 15 minutes till Chinese spinach becomes soft.
- Add salt to taste. Serve hot.

Variations

* The following vegetables can be used in place of Chinese spinach:
(a) 300 g/10 oz Chinese flowering cabbage/mustard leaves (*sawi*).
(b) 150 g/5 oz head cabbage (*kubis*).
(c) 150 g/5 oz Chinese cabbage/Peking cabbage/wong nga pak (*kubis panjang*).

Mixed Vegetable Soup

For Stock

1 rice bowl anchovies (*ikan bilis*)
3 - 4 pieces ginger
1 tbsp oil
840 ml/1½ pt water

Other Ingredients

1 small carrot
1 medium-sized potato
1 tomato
1 onion
salt & pepper to taste

- Prepare stock following method in recipe of Basic Anchovy Stock in this section.
- Dice carrot, potato and onion. Soak potato.
- Cut tomato into wedges.
- Put all the vegetables and stock in the pot. When boiling, lower fire and simmer for 15 minutes.
- Add salt to taste.
- Sprinkle pepper on soup just before serving.

Variation

* You may use basic bone stock in place of basic anchovy stock.

SOUPS

Mungbean Vermicelli Soup with Dried Shrimps and Egg

For Stock

1 rice bowl anchovies (*ikan bilis*)
3 - 4 pieces ginger
1 tbsp oil
840 ml/1½ pt water

Other Ingredients

2 tbsp dried shrimps (*udang kering*)
a few strands of mungbean vermicelli/sohoon
1 egg
1 tsp preserved Chinese cabbage/tong choy – optional
1 pip garlic
1 tbsp oil
salt & pepper to taste

- Prepare stock following method in recipe of Basic Anchovy Stock in this section.
- Wash preserved Chinese cabbage. Cut and soak mungbean vermicelli.
- Wash dried shrimps and strain.
- Chop garlic. Beat egg.
- Heat oil in pot.
- Fry garlic lightly.
- Add in dried shrimps and fry till golden brown.
- Add in stock. When boiling, lower fire and simmer for 15 minutes.
- Add in mungbean vermicelli and preserved Chinese cabbage. Boil for two minutes.
- Lower fire and add in egg, stirring all the time.
- Serve hot.

Angled Luffa Soup

For Stock

1 rice bowl anchovies (*ikan bilis*)
3 - 4 pieces ginger
1 tbsp oil
840 ml/1½ pt water

Other Ingredients

1 angled luffa (*ketola sanding*)
1 piece soft bean curd (*tauhu*)
salt & light soya sauce to taste

- Prepare stock following method in recipe of Basic Anchovy Stock in this section.
- Remove skin from angled luffa and cut according to shape desired.
- Dice soft bean curd into big cubes.
- Put stock, angled luffa and soft bean curd in pot.
- When boiling, lower fire and simmer till angled luffa becomes soft.
- Add salt and light soya sauce. Serve hot.

SOUPS

Salted Vegetable Soup with Soft Bean Curd

For Stock
1 rice bowl anchovies (*ikan bilis*)
3 - 4 pieces ginger
1 tbsp oil
840 ml/1½ pt water

Other Ingredients
150 g/5 oz salted vegetables
2 pieces soft bean curd (*tauhu*)
1 tomato
5 white peppercorns (*lada putih*)
salt to taste

- Separate leaves and stems of salted vegetables. Cut to desired size. Soak in water for 15 minutes.
- Dice soft bean curd into big cubes.
- Cut tomato into wedges.
- Crush peppercorns.
- Prepare stock following method in recipe of Basic Anchovy Stock in this section.
- Squeeze water from salted vegetables.
- Add salted vegetables, tomato and peppercorns to stock. When boiling, lower fire and simmer for 20 minutes.
- Add in soft bean curd and boil for two minutes.
- Add salt to taste. Serve hot.

Variation
* You may use basic bone stock in place of basic anchovy stock.

Chicken Soup

½ chicken
5 white peppercorns (*lada putih*)
1 litre/1¾ pt water
salt to taste

- Remove flesh from chicken and dice.
- Crush peppercorns.
- Put chicken bones, pepper and water in pot.
- When boiling, lower fire and simmer for half an hour. Strain.
- Return stock to pot. When stock boils, add chicken meat and boil for 10 minutes.
- Add salt to taste. Serve hot.

Chicken and Vegetable Soup

½ chicken
1 small carrot
1 medium-sized potato
1 tomato
1 onion
5 white peppercorns (*lada putih*)
1 litre/1¾ pt water

- Cut chicken into suitable-sized pieces.
- Dice carrot, potato and onion. Soak potato.
- Cut tomato in wedges.
- Crush peppercorns.
- Put all the ingredients in the pot.
- When boiling, lower fire and simmer for half an hour.
- Add salt to taste. Serve hot.

Variation
* Ribs can also be used in place of chicken.

SOUPS

Beef Soup

210 g/7 oz beef
4 black peppercorns (*lada hitam*)
1 clove (*bunga cengkih*)
1 star anise (*bunga lawang*)
1 tbsp oil
salt & pepper to taste
840 ml/1½ pt water
1 stick Chinese celery
1 stalk spring onion
fried shallots – amount as desired

- Dice spring onion and beef. Wash spices.
- Crush peppercorns.
- Cut Chinese celery finely.
- Put beef, clove, star anise, pepper and water in pot.
- When boiling, lower fire and simmer for half an hour.
- Add salt to taste.
- Sprinkle pepper, spring onion, Chinese celery and fried shallots on soup. Serve hot.

Mutton Soup

150 g/5 oz mutton
300 g/10 oz mutton bones
2 - 3 pieces ginger
2 cloves (*bunga cengkih*)
5 cm/2" cinnamon (*kayu manis*)
10 black peppercorns (*lada hitam*)
1 litre/1¾ pt water
salt & pepper to taste
1 stick Chinese celery
1 stalk spring onion
fried shallots – amount as desired

- Dice mutton. Season with salt and pepper.
- Shred ginger.
- Crush peppercorns.
- Dice spring onion.
- Cut Chinese celery finely.
- Put water, mutton bones and spices in a pot.
- When boiling, lower fire and simmer for half an hour. Strain.
- Put stock and mutton in the pot.
- When boiling, lower fire and simmer till mutton becomes soft.
- Add salt. Sprinkle spring onion, Chinese celery and fried shallots on soup. Serve hot.

SALAD

TOMATO SALAD **26**

PINEAPPLE SALAD **26**
(KERABU NANAS)

MIXED VEGETABLE SALAD **26**

CUCUMBER SALAD WITH THICK COCONUT MILK **27**
(KERABU TIMUN DENGAN PATI SANTAN)

CUCUMBER SALAD WITH FRIED GRATED COCONUT **27**
(KERABU TIMUN DENGAN KERISIK)

STUFFED EGG SALAD **28**

MALAYSIAN MIXED FRUIT AND VEGETABLE SALAD **30**
(ROJAK)

INDONESIAN MIXED SALAD **32**
(GADO-GADO)

SALAD

Tomato Salad

2 medium-sized tomato
1 onion
1 red chilli
1 stick celery
juice of 2 limes
½ tsp fine sugar
¼ tsp salt
} or to taste

- Dice tomato and onion.
- Shred chilli.
- Slice celery thinly.
- Mix all the ingredients together.
- Taste and serve.

Pineapple Salad (Kerabu Nanas)

½ pineapple
2 - 3 red chillies
3 shallots
1½ cm/½" cube shrimp paste (*belacan*)
1 dsp dried shrimps (*udang kering*)
⅛ tsp salt
⅛ tsp fine sugar or to taste
juice from 1 lime

- Soak dried shrimps.
- Shred pineapple.
- Slice shallots finely lengthwise. Add lime juice.
- Roast shrimp paste till there is nice aroma, then pound it together with chillies. Leave aside.
- Pound dried shrimps.
- Mix all the ingredients together evenly.
- Taste and keep in refrigerator. Serve.

Mixed Vegetable Salad

For Salad
3 pieces salad leaves
½ small yam bean/jicama (*sengkuang*)
¼ small pineapple
1 small carrot
1 tomato
2 tsp frozen peas or tinned peas
1 potato

For Salad Sauce
1 tsp mustard powder (*serbuk biji sawi*)
1 tsp cornflour
3 dsp vinegar
1 dsp sugar
⅛ tsp salt
⅛ tsp pepper
1 tsp margarine
140 ml/¼ pt milk
1 hard-boiled egg – only yolk is used

1 dsp sugar
⅛ tsp salt
⅛ tsp pepper
1 tsp margarine
} or to taste

- Boil potato and dice.
- Prepare sauce following method in recipe of Salad Sauce. Refer to section on Sauces.
- Shred pineapple and salad leaves.
- Dice tomato and yam bean.
- Grate carrot.
- Scald peas.
- Arrange vegetables attractively on plate and serve salad sauce separately; or put all the vegetables in a salad bowl and mix evenly with salad sauce.

SALAD

Cucumber Salad with Thick Coconut Milk
(Kerabu Timun dengan Pati Santan)

1 cucumber
2 shallots
3 red chillies
1½ cm/½" cube shrimp paste (*belacan*)
1 tbsp dried shrimps (*udang kering*)
¼ grated coconut to get 3 - 4 tbsp thick coconut milk
¼ tsp salt or to taste

- Soak dried shrimps.
- Cut cucumber following method as shown in photographs.
- Slice shallots thinly lengthwise.
- Roast shrimp paste till there is nice aroma.
- Pound shrimp paste together with chillies. Leave aside.
- Pound dried shrimps.
- Mix all the ingredients together.
- Taste and serve.

Cucumber Salad with Fried Grated Coconut
(Kerabu Timun dengan Kerisik)

1 cucumber
2 shallots
3 - 4 red chillies
1½ cm/½" cube shrimp paste (*belacan*)
1 tbsp dried shrimps (*udang kering*)
2 tbsp grated white coconut
⅛ tsp salt
⅛ tsp fine sugar   } or to taste
juice of 1 lime

- Soak dried shrimps.
- Fry coconut without oil over low fire, stirring all the time till it is crisp and golden brown.
- Immediately pound fried coconut finely to make *kerisik*. Pounder must be dry.
- Roast shrimp paste till there is nice aroma, then pound it together with chillies. Leave aside.
- Pound dried shrimps.
- Cut cucumber following method as shown in photographs.
- Slice shallots thinly lengthwise.
- Add enough lime juice to taste to cucumber and shallots.
- Mix all the ingredients together evenly.
- Taste and serve.

(i) Remove skin and cut cucumber into 5 cm/2" sections. Slice thinly along length of each section. (Do not use centre).

(ii) Roll up each piece of cucumber and shred finely.

SALAD

Stuffed Egg Salad

For Salad

3 hard-boiled eggs
1 small carrot
1 medium-sized tomato
1 potato
3 salad leaves
1 tsp margarine
⅛ tsp pepper
⅛ tsp salt or to taste
1 red chilli

For Salad Sauce

1 tsp mustard powder (*serbuk biji sawi*)
1 tsp cornflour
3 dsp vinegar
1 dsp sugar
⅛ tsp salt   } or to taste
⅛ tsp pepper
1 tsp margarine
140 ml / ¼ pt milk

- Prepare salad sauce following method in recipe of Salad Sauce. Refer to section on Sauces.
- Cut hard-boiled eggs following method shown in photographs.
- Leave aside egg yolk.
- Boil potato. Mash ¼ potato. Slice remainder of potato.
- Grate carrot.
- Cut tomato in wedges.
- Shred salad leaves.
- Chop red chillies finely.
- Mix ⅔ egg yolk with mashed potato, salt, pepper and mayonnaise. If mixture is too dry, add salad sauce or margarine. Taste.
- Mix the remaining egg yolk with salad sauce.

- Fill egg white with egg mixture.
- Decorate with a little chopped chillies.
- Mix leftover chopped chillies in salad sauce, if desired.
- Arrange all the ingredients attractively on a plate.
- Serve salad and sauce separately.

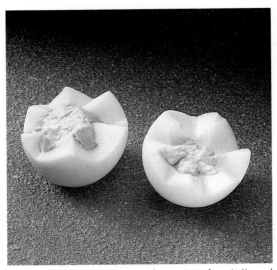

Use a small sharp knife with a pointed end. Stand egg upright. Cut zigzag in the centre to get two halves.

SALAD

Malaysian Mixed Fruit and Vegetable Salad (Rojak)

¼ small pineapple
½ yam bean/jicama (*sengkuang*)
½ cucumber
1 mango – optional
1 rice bowl beansprouts (*tauge*)
2 plants water spinach (*kangkung*)
2 pieces deep-fried bean curd (*tauhu pok*)
2 tbsp groundnuts/peanuts
2 cm/¾" cube shrimp paste (*belacan*)
2 - 3 red chillies
1 dsp prawn paste (*petis*)
1 dsp sweet sauce (*sos manis*) – optional
1 tsp tamarind paste (*asam jawa*)
1 dsp fine sugar
2 tbsp cool boiled water

- Mix boiled water with tamarind paste and strain.
- Fry peanuts without oil using low fire and stirring all the time till peanut skin can be removed easily. Remove skin and pound. Leave aside.
- Pound chillies finely.
- Flatten shrimp paste till 3 mm/⅛" thick. Roast till crispy and nice aroma.
- Immediately mash shrimp paste with a fork into powder form.
- Scald deep-fried bean curd and squeeze out water.
- Scald beansprouts and water spinach separately.
- Cut pineapple, yam bean, cucumber and mango into suitable size and shape.
- Cut water spinach into 2½ cm/1" in length.
- Dice deep-fried bean curd into six cubes.

- Mix tamarind juice with prawn paste, sweet sauce (if used), fine sugar, chillies, powdered shrimp paste and pounded peanuts till sugar dissolves.
- If mixture is too thick, add tamarind juice. Taste.

Suggestions for Serving

* Arrange neatly deep-fried bean curd and all the fruits as well as vegetables on a plate. Serve sauce separately.
* Put ½ amount of fruits, vegetables and deep-fried bean curd in a bowl. Pour sauce over it. Add in the rest of the ingredients and mix thoroughly. Serve.

N.B. Peanuts can be added after mixing fruits in sauce. Then mix evenly. If sweet sauce is left out, increase quantity of sugar to taste.

SALAD

Indonesian Mixed Salad (Gado-gado)

For Salad

1 small yam bean/jicama (*sengkuang*)
½ cucumber
2 head cabbage leaves (*kubis*)
2 plants water spinach (*kangkung*)
4 long beans
1 rice bowl beansprouts (*tauge*)
1 medium-sized potato
2 pieces hard bean curd (*taukua*)
2 hard-boiled eggs
a few crackers – optional

For Salad Sauce

4 shallots
4 - 6 dried chillies
2 cm/¾" cube shrimp paste (*belacan*)
1 dsp tamarind paste (*asam jawa*) or to taste
½ grated coconut to get 140 ml/¼ pt thick coconut milk
1 tsp chopped palm sugar (*gula melaka*)
¼ tsp salt or to taste
3 tbsp oil
2 tbsp groundnuts/peanuts

- Mix tamarind paste with 2 tbsp water. Strain.
- Fry peanuts without oil over low fire, stirring all the time till peanut skin can be removed easily. Remove skin and pound finely.
- Roast shrimp paste till there is nice aroma.
- Pound finely shallots, chillies and roasted shrimp paste.
- Heat oil in wok.
- Fry hard bean curd till golden brown. Leave aside.

- Fry chilli mixture till oil appears.
- Add ½ amount of thick coconut milk and pounded peanuts, little by little, stirring all the time. Simmer till oil appears.
- Add in leftover coconut milk, tamarind juice, palm sugar and salt. Stir evenly and simmer for five minutes. Taste.
- Slice hard-boiled eggs.
- Boil potato. Remove skin and slice.
- Cut long beans. Shred yam bean and cucumber.
- Scald head cabbage, long beans, beansprouts and water spinach separately.
- Cut head cabbage and water spinach.
- Dice hard bean curd into cubes.
- Arrange vegetables, eggs and hard bean curd attractively on a plate.
- Serve sauce separately.
- Serve crackers on a plate.

ONE - DISH MEAL

PLAIN PORRIDGE – BASIC RECIPE 34

FISH PORRIDGE 34

MEAT PORRIDGE 35

SPICY PORRIDGE 35

FRIED RICE 36

SPICY FRIED RICE 36

LENTIL RICE 37
(NASI PARPU)

COCONUT MILK RICE WITH ANCHOVY SAMBAL 38
(NASI LEMAK DENGAN SAMBAL IKAN BILIS)

TURMERIC GLUTINOUS RICE WITH MEAT RENDANG 41
(NASI KUNYIT DENGAN RENDANG DAGING)

FRIED RICE NOODLES/FRIED MEEHOON 42
(MIHUN GORENG)

FRIED VEGETARIAN RICE NOODLES/FRIED VEGETARIAN MEEHOON 43

FRIED RICE NOODLES SIAMESE STYLE 44
(MI SIAM)

RICE NOODLES WITH SALAD/MEEHOON WITH SALAD 45
(KERABU MIHUN)

FRIED WHEAT NOODLES/FRIED MEE 46
(MI GORENG)

FRIED FLAT RICE NOODLES/FRIED KWAY TEOW 47
(KUETIAU GORENG)

FLAT RICE NOODLES SOUP/KWAY TEOW SOUP 48
(SUP KUETIAU)

WHEAT FLOUR VERMICELLI SOUP 49
(SUP MI SUAH)

LAKSA NOODLES IN TAMARIND SOUP 50
(LAKSA ASAM)

MACARONI PIE 52

FRIED MACARONI 54

SPAGHETTI WITH TOMATO SAUCE 54

ONE - DISH MEAL

Plain Porridge – Basic Recipe

1 - 2 tbsp rice
560 ml/1 pt water
¼ tsp salt ⎫ to season
1 tsp oil ⎭ rice

- Wash rice. Season rice with oil and salt for at least half an hour.
- Add water and put to boil.
- When boiling, lower fire. Simmer till rice becomes soft and broken.
- Stir once in a while when simmering. Add salt if necessary. Taste and serve.

N.B. Quantity in this recipe is enough for one person only.

Fish Porridge

1 - 2 tbsp rice
560 ml/1 pt water
¼ tsp salt ⎫ to season
1 tsp oil ⎭ rice
90 g/3 oz fish
2 slices ginger
1 dsp oil
1 dsp light soya sauce
⅛ tsp pepper
1 stalk spring onion
fried shallots – optional

- Cook porridge. Refer to basic recipe for porridge in this section.
- Slice fish thinly. Shred ginger.
- Season fish with ginger, light soya sauce, pepper and oil.
- When porridge is ready, add in fish. Stir to mix well. Simmer for one minute till fish is cooked. Add salt and taste.
- Sprinkle chopped spring onion, fried shallots and pepper on porridge before serving.

Variation
* You may use oats to cook the porridge in place of rice.

N.B. Quantity in this recipe is enough for one person only.

ONE - DISH MEAL

Meat Porridge

1 - 2 tbsp rice
560 ml/1 pt water
¼ tsp salt   } to season
1 tsp oil   } rice
90 g/3 oz meat
1 dsp light soya sauce
1 tsp oil
¼ tsp cornflour
1 stalk spring onion
fried shallots – optional

- Cook porridge. Refer to basic recipe for porridge in this section.
- Mince meat and add soya sauce, pepper, cornflour and oil. Mix evenly.
- Make meat balls.
- When porridge is ready, add in meat balls. Stir porridge. When porridge boils, lower fire and simmer for two minutes till meat balls are cooked. Add salt and taste.
- Sprinkle chopped spring onion, fried shallots and pepper on porridge before serving.

Variation

* Use oats to cook porridge in place of rice.

N.B. Quantity in this recipe is enough for one person only.

Spicy Porridge

120 g/4 oz rice
1 litre/1¾ pt water
½ tsp salt
150 g/5 oz meat
1 tbsp light soya sauce }
½ tsp cornflour   } to season
⅛ tsp pepper   } rice
10 black peppercorns
¼ star anise (*bunga lawang*)
2 cloves (*bunga cengkih*)
2½ cm/1" length cinnamon (*kayu manis*)
3 tbsp oil
1 stalk spring onion
1 sprig Chinese celery
4 shallots

- Wash rice and strain. Slice shallots finely.
- Heat 3 tbsp oil in a pot. Fry shallots till golden brown. Dish out.
- Fry pepper, star anise, cloves and cinnamon till nice aroma.
- Add in rice and mix well. Add water.
- When boiling, lower fire and simmer till rice is soft and broken. Stir occasionally.
- Dice meat into small cubes. Season with light soya sauce, pepper and cornflour.
- When porridge is ready, add in meat. Stir and mix well. Boil for another three to five minutes. When meat is cooked, add salt. Taste.
- Cut spring onion and Chinese celery finely. Sprinkle spring onion, celery, fried shallots (if used) and pepper on porridge before serving.

N.B. This quantity serves three to four persons.

ONE - DISH MEAL

Fried Rice

2 rice bowls cooked rice – cooled
150 g/5 oz prawns
4 long beans or 6 French beans
(*kacang buncis*)
½ small carrot
2 pips garlic
1 egg
1 dsp light soya sauce
salt & pepper to taste
3 tbsp oil
egg omelette – optional
fried shallots – optional

- Season prawns with salt and pepper.
- Chop garlic. Dice carrot and French beans.
- Heat 2 tbsp oil, add garlic. Fry till golden brown.
- Add prawns, fry for a while. Add carrot, French beans and salt. Fry for one minute.
- Add in rice and light soya sauce. Mix well.
- Make a well in the centre of rice. Add in 1 tbsp oil. Break in egg. Add in ½ tsp light soya sauce. Cover egg with rice for one minute. Stir and mix well. Taste.
- Garnish with fried shallots, sliced chillies and egg omelette strips before serving.

Variations
* You may use 2 tbsp dried shrimps (*udang kering*) in place of prawns.
* Use peas in place of beans.

Spicy Fried Rice

2 rice bowls cooked rice – cooled
½ small carrot
4 long beans
2 tbsp dried shrimps (*udang kering*)
4 shallots
4 red chillies
1½ cm/½" cube shrimp paste (*belacan*)
1 tbsp light soya sauce
½ tsp thick soya sauce
4 tbsp oil
2 eggs
¼ tsp pepper   } or to
¼ tsp salt   } taste
¼ cucumber

- Soak dried chillies and dried shrimps separately.
- Pound together chillies, shallots and shrimp paste. Leave aside.
- Strain dried shrimps and pound.
- Heat oil. Fry chilli mixture till there is nice aroma.
- Add dried shrimps. Fry for a while. Add carrot and long beans. Fry for one minute. Add 1 tbsp water if necessary.
- Add in rice and soya sauce. Mix well. Add a little water if necessary.
- Make a well in the centre of rice. Add in 1 tbsp oil. Break in eggs. Add in pepper and salt.
- Cover eggs with rice for one minute. Stir to mix well. Taste.
- Garnish with sliced cucumber before serving.

ONE - DISH MEAL

Lentil Rice (Nasi Parpu)

60 g/2 oz lentils (*kacang dal*) soaked for at
least 4 hours
180 g/6 oz rice
560 ml/1 pt water
2½ cm/1" length cinnamon (*kayu manis*)
4 cloves (*bunga cengkih*)
4 shallots
1 tbsp raisins
3 tbsp oil
½ tsp salt
½ carrot
4 French beans (*kacang buncis*)

- Wash rice and strain. Wash lentils and strain.
- Slice shallots thinly. Dice carrot and French beans.

- Heat oil. Fry shallots till golden brown. Dish out. Fry raisins. Dish out.
- Add in cinnamon and cloves. Fry till there is nice aroma. Add lentils, rice and salt. Mix well.
- Add in water. Mix thoroughly. Allow to boil. When water is nearly drying up, add carrot and French beans. Cook for another five to 10 minutes with low fire till cooked.
- Garnish with fried shallots and raisins.

Suggestions for Serving

* You may serve with the following dishes:
(a) Lentil curry or hard bean curd *sambal* (*sambal taukua*) – Refer to section on Vegetarian Dishes.
(b) Anchovy sambal with *belimbing* fruit (*sambal ikan bilis dengan buah belimbing besi*) or fish curry – Refer to section on Fish.
(c) Meat curry – Refer to section on Meat.

ONE - DISH MEAL

Coconut Milk Rice with Anchovy Sambal (Nasi Lemak dengan Sambal Ikan Bilis)

For Coconut Rice

240 g/8 oz rice
½ grated coconut to get 420 ml/¾ pt
coconut milk
½ tsp salt
2 screwpine leaves/*pandan* leaves
2 eggs
½ cucumber

For Anchovy *Sambal*

3 tbsp anchovies (*ikan bilis*)
½ onion
4 dried chillies
4 shallots
1 stick lemon grass (*serai*)
2 cm/¾" cube shrimp paste (*belacan*)
1 tsp tamarind paste (*asam jawa*)
3 - 4 tbsp water
3 tbsp oil
¼ tsp salt ⎫ or to
½ tsp sugar ⎭ taste

Other Ingredient

4 - 6 banana leaves measuring 20¼ cm × 25½ cm/8" × 10" rectangle – softened.

Preparation of Coconut Milk Rice

- Prepare steamer.
- Wash and strain rice into steaming tray.
- Add coconut milk, salt, eggs and screwpine leaves.
- Steam for 20 - 30 minutes till cooked.
- Remove eggs and screwpine leaves.
- Fluff up the rice.

Preparation of Anchovy *Sambal*

- Soak dried chillies.
- Slice lemon grass. Slice onion into rings.
- Roast shrimp paste.
- Pound chillies, lemon grass, shallots and shrimp paste finely.
- Mix tamarind paste with water and strain.
- Wash and wipe anchovies dry.
- Heat oil. Fry anchovies over low fire, stirring all the time. Dish out when golden brown.
- Fry pounded ingredients till there is nice aroma and oil appears. Add onion. Mix well.
- Add tamarind juice, sugar and salt. Simmer for five minutes. Taste.
- Add anchovies. Mix well. Turn off fire.

To Wrap Coconut Rice

- Slice cucumber. Cut eggs into wedges.
- Divide rice and *sambal* into four to six portions. Put one portion of rice on banana leaf.
- Arrange pieces of cucumber, egg and anchovy *sambal* on the rice. Wrap up the rice.

Variations in Serving

* Dish one portion of rice on a plate. Arrange cucumber, egg and anchovy *sambal* on it.
* Serve rice, anchovy *sambal*, egg and cucumber separately.

Other Suggestion for Serving

* Serve coconut milk rice with chilli shrimp paste sauce (*sambal belacan*) and fried prawns with tamarind paste (*udang asam goreng*). You may refer to section on Sauces and Fish.

ONE - DISH MEAL

Turmeric Glutinous Rice with Meat Rendang (Nasi Kunyit dengan Rendang Daging)

For Turmeric Glutinous Rice

300 g/10 oz glutinous rice (*pulut*).
1 tsp turmeric powder (*serbuk kunyit*)
2 pieces dried tamarind skins (*asam gelugur*)
½ grated coconut to get 280 ml/½ pt coconut milk
½ tsp salt or to taste
10 black peppercorns
3 cloves (*bunga cengkih*)

For Meat *Rendang*/Spicy Meat in Coconut Milk

300 g/10 oz beef or mutton
1 grated coconut to get 1 litre/1¾ pt coconut milk
8 - 10 dried chillies
8 shallots
2 pips garlic
2 sticks lemon grass (*serai*)
1 piece ginger (1½ cm/½" thick)
1 turmeric leaf (*daun kunyit*) – optional
1 slice galangal (*lengkuas*)
2 pieces dried tamarind skins (*asam gelugur*)
½ tsp salt or to taste
1 tomato
½ cucumber

Preparation of Turmeric Glutinous Rice

- Wash glutinous rice. Add in 980 ml/1¾ pt water. Add turmeric powder and dried tamarind skins. Mix thoroughly. Leave for at least four hours so that rice turns yellow colour.

- Strain glutinous rice into a steaming tray. Add black peppercorns, cloves and salt. Pour in enough coconut milk just to cover the rice.
- Steam for 20 - 30 minutes till cooked. Loosen rice with ladle.

Suggestion for Serving

* To shape glutinous rice for serving, first wet a suitable mould.
* Put in rice and press firmly with a wooden spoon.
* Overturn the mould on a plate and shake mould to loosen glutinous rice from mould.
* Decorate the side of plate with cucumber and tomato.
* Serve with meat *rendang* separately.

Preparation of Meat *Rendang*

- Refer to recipe of Meat *Rendang*/Spicy Meat in Coconut Milk (*Rendang Daging*). Refer to section on Meat.

Variations in Serving

* Serve turmeric glutinous rice with meat curry or fried spicy meat (*daging goreng berempah*) and pickled cucumber (*acar timun*) – Refer to section on Meat and Preserves.

ONE - DISH MEAL

Fried Rice Noodles/Fried Meehoon (Mihun Goreng)

240 g/8 oz rice noodles/meehoon
150 g/5 oz prawns
¼ tsp sugar
¼ tsp pepper
90 g/3 oz Chinese flowering cabbage/
mustard leaves (*sawi*)
1 rice bowl beansprouts (*tauge*)
3 pips garlic
3 tbsp oil
1 tbsp light soya sauce ⎫
1 tsp thick soya sauce ⎬ or to
⅛ tsp pepper ⎪ taste
¼ tsp salt ⎭
egg omelette – optional
fried shallots – optional
1 red chilli

- Season prawns with ¼ tsp sugar and ⅛ tsp pepper.
- Soak rice noodles in water. Strain when soft.
- Chop garlic. Cut mustard leaves.
- Heat 1 tbsp oil. Fry garlic till golden brown. Add prawns. Fry for a few minutes and dish out.
- Add in mustard leaves and fry for a while. Add in beansprouts. Mix well. Dish out.
- Heat 1 tbsp oil. Fry remaining ⅔ garlic till golden brown. Add rice noodles, sauces, salt and pepper. Stir to mix evenly.
- Sprinkle a little water over rice noodles if dry.
- Add in prawns and vegetables. Mix well. Taste.
- Garnish rice noodles with egg omelette, fried shallots and red chilli.
- Serve with chilli sauce desired. Refer to section on Sauces.

ONE - DISH MEAL

Fried Vegetarian Rice Noodles/ Fried Vegetarian Meehoon

240 g/8 oz rice noodles/meehoon

1 small carrot

4 head cabbage leaves (*daun kubis*)

2 pieces hard bean curd (*taukua*)

2 pieces black fungi/mok yee – optional

2 pieces dried sweet bean curd sheets (*timcuk*)

1½ tbsp light soya sauce

½ tsp thick soya sauce

¼ tsp salt   } or to

½ tsp pepper   taste

4 tbsp oil

2 shallots

1 red chilli

- Soak black fungi if used.
- Soak rice noodles in water. Strain when soft.
- Wipe dry sweet bean curd sheets with dry cloth. Cut crosswise into 6 cm/¼" strips.
- Wash and wipe dry hard bean curd. Cut into strips.
- Slice and shred carrot.
- Slice shallots.
- Shred head cabbage leaves, chilli and black fungi.
- Heat oil. Fry shallots till golden brown. Dish out.
- Fry dried sweet bean curd strips till golden brown. Dish out.
- Fry hard bean curd till golden brown. Dish out.
- Add carrot, head cabbage, black fungi and salt. Fry for one minute. Add rice noodles and sauces, stirring to mix well.
- Add in hard bean curd. Taste.
- Garnish rice noodles with fried shallots, red chillies and dried sweet bean curd strips.
- Serve with chilli sauce desired. Refer to section on Sauces.

ONE - DISH MEAL

Fried Rice Noodles Siamese Style (Mi Siam)

240 g/8 oz rice noodles/meehoon
150 g/5 oz prawns
¼ tsp sugar
⅛ tsp pepper
1 rice bowl beansprouts (*tauge*)
2 stalks Chinese chives (*kucai*)
1 piece hard bean curd (*taukua*)
4 shallots
4 red chillies
4 dried chillies
4 tbsp oil
1 tbsp light soya sauce
2 hard-boiled eggs
2 limes

For Soyabean Paste Sauce (Sos Taucu)

1 tbsp soyabean paste (taucu)
1 pip garlic
⅛ tsp pepper
1 tsp sugar
¼ tsp salt   } mix together
½ tsp cornflour
4 tbsp water
1 tbsp oil

- Soak dried chillies in hot water.
- Soak rice noodles in water. Strain when soft.

- Season prawns with sugar and pepper.
- Cut chives. Wipe dry hard bean curd and dice.
- Cut limes and eggs into wedges or slices.
- Chop garlic and soyabean paste separately.
- Pound dried chillies, red chillies and shallots finely.
- Heat 2 tbsp oil. Fry hard bean curd till golden brown. Dish out.

Preparation of Soyabean Paste Sauce

- Fry garlic till there is nice aroma. Add soyabean paste. Fry for a while.
- Add cornflour mixture. Mix well. Simmer for one minute. Taste. Serve in a bowl.

Preparation of Fried Rice Noodles Siamese Style

- Heat 2 tbsp oil. Fry pounded ingredients till there is nice aroma and oil appears. Add prawns and fry for a short while.
- Add beansprouts. Fry for a few minutes.
- Add in rice noodles and light soya sauce mixture, stirring to mix well. Sprinkle water on rice noodles if it is too dry. Add in Chinese chives. Mix well. Taste.
- Dish out and garnish with slices or wedges of limes and eggs. Serve with sauce separately.

44

ONE - DISH MEAL

Rice Noodles with Salad/Meehoon with Salad (Kerabu Mihun)

240 g/8 oz rice noodles/meehoon
150 g/5 oz prawns
1 rice bowl beansprouts (*tauge*)
4 stalks Chinese chives (*kucai*)
2 pieces black fungus/mok yee – optional
10 lime leaves (*daun limau purut*) – optional
¼ grated white coconut or 2 - 3 tbsp
desiccated coconut
10 shallots
lime juice from 10 limes or to taste
10 red chillies
2½ cm/1" cube shrimp paste (*belacan*)
½ tsp salt or to taste
2 hard-boiled eggs

- Soak rice noodles in water. Strain when soft.
- Soak black fungi if used.
- Dice eggs.
- Boil prawns without removing shell.
- When cooked, shell prawns and slice thinly.
- Slice shallots lengthwise. Shred lime leaves finely.
- Scald black fungi, beansprouts, chives and rice noodles separately.
- Shred black fungi finely. Cut chives.
- Fry grated coconut without oil over low fire, stirring all the time till golden brown and crispy.
- Immediately after that, pound grated coconut finely using dry pounder. Do not fry if desiccated coconut is used.
- Roast shrimp paste till there is nice aroma.

- Pound shrimp paste with red chillies.
- Mix together enough lime juice, chilli mixture, ½ tsp salt and shallots evenly.
- Put ½ amount of rice noodles in a mixing bowl. Add in chilli mixture, eggs, prawns, beansprouts, Chinese chives, lime leaves, black fungi and pounded coconut or desiccated coconut.
- Add in remaining rice noodles.
- Stir to mix evenly.
- Serve.

ONE - DISH MEAL

Fried Wheat Noodles/Fried Mee (Mi Goreng)

240 g/8 oz wheat noodles/mee
150 g/5 oz prawns
½ tsp sugar
⅛ tsp pepper
1 rice bowl beansprouts (*tauge*)
90 g/3 oz Chinese flowering cabbage/
mustard leaves (*sawi*)
3 pips garlic
3 tbsp oil
½ tsp thick soya sauce
1 tbsp light soya sauce ⎫
½ tsp salt   ⎬ mixed together
⅛ tsp pepper   ⎪
¼ tsp cornflour ⎭
chilli shrimp paste sauce
(*sambal belacan*)
egg omelette
fried shallots
1 red chilli

- Season prawns with sugar and pepper.
- Chop garlic and cut mustard leaves.
- Rinse wheat noodles under tap water just before frying.
- Heat 2 tbsp oil. Fry ½ amount of garlic till golden brown. Add in prawns and fry for one minute. Dish out.
- Heat 1 tbsp oil. Fry remaining garlic till golden brown. Add in mustard leaves. Fry till soft. Add a little water if necessary.
- Add beansprouts. Stir well. Add seasoning, prawns and wheat noodles. Add a little water if necessary. Mix evenly. Taste.
- Garnish wheat noodles with egg omelette, fried shallots and red chilli.
- Serve with chilli shrimp paste sauce (*sambal belacan*).

ONE - DISH MEAL

Fried Flat Rice Noodles/Fried Kway Teow (Kuetiau Goreng)

2 pieces flat rice noodles/kway teow
(*kuetiau*)
150 g/5 oz prawns
¼ tsp sugar ⎫ to season
⅛ tsp pepper ⎭ prawns
1 rice bowl beansprouts (*tauge*)
2 stalks Chinese chives (*kucai*)
2 pips garlic
3 - 4 red chillies or to taste
1 tbsp light soya sauce
½ tsp thick soya sauce – optional
2 - 3 eggs
¼ tsp salt or to taste
4 tbsp oil

- Season prawns with sugar and pepper.
- Cut Chinese chives. Chop garlic. Cut flat rice noodles into strips.

- Pound chillies finely.
- Heat 2 tbsp oil. Fry garlic till golden brown.
- Add prawns. Fry for a while. Add chillies and fry with prawns. Add beansprouts. Fry for a while. Add flat rice noodles and sauce. Fry for several minutes and mix well.
- Make a well in the centre of flat rice noodles, add in 1 tbsp oil.
- Break in eggs and ½ tbsp soya sauce, pepper and salt. Cover egg with flat rice noodles for one minute.
- Add in Chinese chives and stir to mix well. Taste and serve.

Variations

* Rice noodles/meehoon, macaroni or wheat noodles/mee can also be fried with this method.

ONE - DISH MEAL

Flat Rice Noodles Soup/Kway Teow Soup (Sup Kuetiau)

2 - 3 pieces flat rice noodles/
kway teow (*kuetiau*)
240 g/8 oz fish
4 slices ginger
1 tsp oil
1 dsp light soya sauce
½ tsp pepper
½ tsp salt or to taste
150 g/5 oz Chinese flowering cabbage/
mustard leaves (*sawi*)

For Basic Anchovy Stock
1 rice bowl anchovies (*ikan bilis*)
3 - 4 slices ginger
1 tbsp oil
840 ml/1½ pt water
fried shallots – optional
chillies

- Prepare stock following method in recipe of Basic Anchovy Stock.
- Slice fish thinly.
- Shred ginger.
- Cut flat rice noodles into strips.
- Season fish with ginger, light soya sauce, pepper and oil.
- Separate mustard leaves from stem and cut into 2" lengths. Scald till soft.
- Scald flat rice noodles.
- Add fish and ½ tsp salt to stock. Simmer for a while. Taste.
- Put some flat rice noodles and vegetables into a bowl.
  Pour soup and some fish over the flat rice noodles.
- Garnish with fried shallots and chillies. Serve hot.

Variations
* You may use fish balls, meat cut into thin slices or minced meat balls in place of fish.
* Use scalded beansprouts (*tauge*) in place of mustard leaves.
* Rice noodles/meehoon, wheat noodles/mee, mungbean vermicelli/sohoon or macaroni can also be cooked with this mathod.

ONE - DISH MEAL

Wheat Flour Vermicelli Soup (Sup Mi Suah)

2 bundles wheat flour vermicelli (*mi suah*)
2 tbsp oil
½ tsp salt

For Basic Bone Stock

90 g/3 oz bones
2 peppercorns
280 ml/½ pt water

For Meat Balls

90 g/3 oz meat
1 dsp light soya sauce
⅛ tsp pepper
¼ tsp cornflour
fried shallots
1 stalk spring onion

- Prepare bone stock following method in recipe of Basic Bone Stock in section on Soups.
- Mince meat finely.
- Season meat with light soya sauce, pepper and cornflour. Shape meat into balls.
- Scald wheat flour vermicelli. Rinse in cooled boiled water. Strain and mix with 1 tbsp oil.
- Boil stock in a pot.
- Add meat balls.
- When meat balls are cooked, add wheat flour vermicelli. Add salt and taste.
- Garnish with fried shallots and spring onion. Serve hot.

Variation

* You may cook macaroni in the same way.

ONE - DISH MEAL

Laksa Noodles in Tamarind Soup (Laksa Asam)

240 g/8 oz fresh *laksa* noodles
240 g/8 oz mackerals (*ikan kembung*)
1 litre/1¾ pt water
½ tsp salt
8 dried chillies
2 sticks lemon grass (*serai*)
2 pips garlic
2½ cm/1" cube shrimp paste (*belacan*)
2½ cm/1" turmeric (*kunyit*)
6 - 8 pieces dried
tamarind skins (*asam gelugur*)
4 sprigs annatto leaves (*daun kesum*) –
optional
4 salad leaves
½ cucumber
2 sprigs mint leaves (*daun pudina*)
¼ pineapple
1 onion
1 ginger flower (*bunga kantan*)
2 green chillies
2 red chillies
2 tbsp prawn paste (*petis*)
2 limes

- Soak dried chillies.
- Boil fish with 1 litre water.
- Slice lemon grass.
- Pound together dried chillies, lemon grass, turmeric, garlic, shallots and shrimp paste.

- When fish is cooked remove fish from stock.
- Add in chilli mixture, ½ tsp salt, dried tamarind skins and annatto leaves.
- Mix well and simmer for 20 minutes.
- Remove bones from fish and mash.
- After simmering chilli mixture for 20 minutes, remove annatto leaves and dried tamarind skins. Add in fish. Simmer for a short while. Taste.
- Scald fresh *laksa* noodles quickly.
- Slice salad leaves, onion and ginger flower.
- Slice and shred cucumber.
- Shred green chillies, red chillies and pineapple.
- Cut limes in halves crosswise.
- Pluck mint leaves from stem.
- Arrange all the vegetables separately on a plate.
- Mix prawn paste with 1 dsp boiled water and serve separately.
- Put *laksa* noodles in a plate.

Suggestion for Serving

* Place required amount of *laksa* noodles in a bowl. Add vegetables desired and enough prawn paste to taste. Pour hot soup over ingredients.

Variations

* Rice noodles/meehoon including thick meehoon or wheat noodles/mee can also be used in place of fresh *laksa* noodles.

ONE - DISH MEAL

Macaroni Pie

60 g/2 oz macaroni
1 tsp salt
3 eggs
¼ tsp pepper
140 ml/¼ pt milk or coconut milk
1 onion
90 g/3 oz meat
1 dsp light soya sauce
¼ tsp pepper
¼ tsp cornflour
3 tbsp oil or 1 tbsp margarine
1 sprig Chinese celery
3 pieces ginger
4 shallots
1 cm/⅜" cinnamon (*kayu manis*)
1 cardamom (*buah pelaga*)
1 clove (*bunga cengkih*)
⅛ star anise (*bunga lawang*)
1 stalk spring onion
chilli sauce or barbecue sauce

- Boil 840 ml/1½ pt water with 1 tsp salt.
- Add macaroni and boil for 10-15 minutes till soft. Strain and rinse under tap water.
- Cut meat into small cubes.

- Season with light soya sauce, pepper and cornflour.
- Dice onion. Shred Chinese celery.
- Pound finely cinnamon, cardamom, clove and star anise. Add ginger and shallots. Pound finely.
- Beat eggs with ¼ tsp salt and ¼ tsp pepper.
- Mix together with milk or coconut milk.
- Heat oil or margarine and fry pounded spices till there is nice aroma.
- Add in meat and onion. Fry for one minute.
- Add in macaroni and mix well. Taste.
- Add in Chinese celery and mix well. Dish out. Cool macaroni slightly.
- Mix in egg mixture.
- Put mixture in a greased pyrex dish and bake in 150°C/300°F/2 for 20-30 minutes. Cool before cutting.
- Garnish with spring onion and serve with chilli sauce or barbecue sauce separately. Refer to section on Sauces.

Suggestion

* You may use ½ tsp mixed spice powder or five spice powder/goh heong hun/ng heong fun in place of spices mentioned above.

ONE - DISH MEAL

Fried Macaroni

180 g/6 oz macaroni
1 litre/1¾ pt water
1 tsp salt
90 g/3 oz meat
1 dsp light soya sauce
⅛ tsp pepper
¼ tsp cornflour
2 eggs
½ carrot
6 French beans (*kacang buncis*)
2 pips garlic
3 red chillies
3 tbsp oil
1 stalk spring onion
½ tsp salt

- Boil 1 litre water with 1 tsp salt.
- When water boils, add in macaroni and simmer for 10 - 15 minutes till soft. Strain and rinse under tap water.
- Cut meat into small cubes.
- Season with light soya sauce and cornflour.
- Pound chillies finely.
- Slice garlic. Dice carrot and French beans.
- Beat eggs with salt and pepper.
- Heat oil. Fry garlic for a while.
- Add in chillies and fry for a while.
- Add meat. Fry for two minutes.
- If mixture is dry, add 1 - 2 tbsp water.
- Add in carrot, French beans and salt. Fry for one minute.
- Add macaroni and mix well.
- Make a well in the centre of the macaroni mixture and pour eggs into well.
- Cover eggs with macaroni for one minute. Stir and mix well.
- Garnish with spring onion and serve.

Variation

* Mix 1 tbsp tomato sauce to the chilli mixture when frying chillies.

Spaghetti with Tomato Sauce

180 g/6 oz spaghetti
1 litre/1¾ pt water
1 tsp salt
1 dsp margarine/butter
90 g/3 oz minced meat
1 tbsp light soya sauce
¼ tsp pepper
¼ tsp cornflour
1 onion
½ carrot
2 tbsp peas
2 tbsp oil
3 - 4 tbsp tomato sauce or to taste

- Boil water with salt.
- When water boils, immerse spaghetti in the boiling water. Do not cover saucepan. Simmer spaghetti for 20 - 30 minutes till cooked.
- Drain cooked spaghetti and mix with margarine.
- Mix minced meat with light soya sauce, pepper and cornflour.
- Dice onion and carrot.
- Heat oil. Sauté onion. Add carrot and meat. Sauté for a while. Add tomato sauce. Fry lightly for a few minutes. If too dry add a little water.
- Mix in peas.
- When vegetables and meat are cooked, add spaghetti. Stir well.
- Taste before serving.

VEGETABLES

HEAD CABBAGE IN COCONUT MILK 56
(KUBIS MASAK LEMAK)

FRIED MUSTARD LEAVES WITH PRAWNS 56

FRIED MIXED VEGETABLES 57

FRIED BEANSPROUTS WITH SALTED FISH 57

FRIED LARGE BEANSPROUTS WITH MINCED MEAT 58

FRIED WATER SPINACH WITH CHILLI SHRIMP PASTE SAUCE 58
(KANGKUNG GORENG SAMBAL BELACAN)

FRIED ANGLED LUFFA OMELETTE 60

FRIED DICED LONG BEANS 60

VEGETABLE CURRY 62

GRILLED BRINJALS 64

VEGETABLE CUTLETS 64

VEGETABLES

Head Cabbage in Coconut Milk (Kubis Masak Lemak)

300 g/10 oz head cabbage (*kubis*)
1 red chilli
½ sweet potato – optional
1 tbsp dried shrimps (*udang kering*)
½ grated coconut to get 420 ml/¾ pt
coconut milk
4 shallots
¼ tsp salt or to taste

- Soak dried shrimps.
- Shred head cabbage. Slice red chilli and shallots.
- Strain dried shrimps and pound.
- Put all the ingredients in a pot and boil till cabbage becomes soft.
- Taste and serve.

Variations

* You may use 150 g/5 oz prawns in place of dried shrimps.
* Any one or a combination of the following vegetables can be used in place of head cabbage: Chinese spinach (*bayam*), edible ferns (*pucuk paku*), Chinese flowering cabbage/mustard leaves (*sawi*) or water spinach (*kangkung*).

Fried Mustard Leaves with Prawns

300 g/10 oz Chinese flowering cabbage/
mustard leaves (*sawi*)
120 g/4 oz prawns
1 pip garlic
1 shallot
2 tbsp oil
1 tsp light soya sauce ⎫
¼ tsp salt ⎬ or to taste
⅛ tsp pepper ⎭
¼ tsp sugar

- Season prawns with sugar and pepper.
- Separate mustard leaves from stems. Cut into 5 cm/2" lengths separately.
- Slice shallots and chop garlic.
- Heat oil. Sauté garlic and shallots till golden brown.
- Add prawns and sauté for one minute.
- Add stems and sauté for one minute.
- Add leaves and sauté for one minute.
- Add 2 tbsp water and fry till vegetables become soft.
- Add salt and light soya sauce. Mix well. Taste.
- Sprinkle some pepper on top and serve.

Variations

* Any one of the following vegetables can be used in place of mustard leaves: French beans, long beans, head cabbage, Chinese spinach (*bayam*) or water spinach (*kangkung*).

VEGETABLES

Fried Mixed Vegetables

150 g/5 oz prawns
¼ cauliflower
5 cm/2" carrot
8 French beans (*kacang buncis*) or
30 g/1 oz peas
1 capsicum – optional
3 pips garlic
4 tbsp oil
1 tbsp light soya sauce
3 tbsp water
¼ tsp salt ⎫
¼ tsp sugar ⎬ or to taste
⅛ tsp pepper ⎭

- Season prawns with sugar and pepper.
- Chop garlic.
- Cut cauliflower and French beans.
- Cut carrot to desired shape.
- Remove seeds from capsicum and cut into eight sections.
- Heat 1 tbsp oil and sauté ¼ quantity of garlic till golden brown. Add cauliflower. Mix well. Add 1 tsp light soya sauce and 1 tbsp water. Fry for one minute. Dish out.
- Repeat the above process with carrot and capsicum.
- Heat oil and sauté remaining garlic till golden brown.
- Add prawns and fry for one minute. Add French beans or peas and fry for one minute.
- Add the other vegetables and salt. Mix well.
- Taste and serve.

Variation
* Celery and meat can also be added.

Fried Beansprouts with Salted Fish

300 g/10 oz beansprouts (*tauge*)
30 g/1 oz salted fish
1 stalk Chinese chives (*kucai*)
1 red chilli
2 pips garlic
2 tbsp oil
1 tsp light soya sauce ⎫ or to
⅛ tsp pepper ⎬ taste

- Cut salted fish into small cubes.
- Cut Chinese chives into 5 cm/2" lengths.
- Shred chilli and chop garlic.
- Heat 1 tbsp oil and sauté ½ quantity garlic till golden brown.
- Add salted fish. Sauté fish till golden brown and crispy. Dish out.
- Heat 1 tbsp oil and sauté remaining garlic till golden brown.
- Add chilli and Chinese chives. Fry for one minute.
- Add beansprouts and fry for one minute.
- Add salted fish and light soya sauce. Mix well. Dish out.
- Sprinkle pepper and serve.

VEGETABLES

Fried Large Beansprouts with Minced Meat

300 g/10 oz large beansprouts
(*tauge kasar*)
150 g/5 oz minced meat
2 pips garlic
2 tbsp oil
¼ tsp salt
1 tsp light soya sauce } or to taste
⅛ tsp pepper

- Season minced meat with light soya sauce.
- Chop large beansprouts and garlic separately.
- Fry large beansprouts without oil using low fire till almost dry. Dish out.
- Heat oil. Sauté garlic till golden brown.
- Add minced meat and sauté for one minute.
- Add large beansprouts and sauté well for one minute.
- Add salt and taste. Dish out.
- Sprinkle pepper on top and serve.

Variation
* You may use 150 g/5 oz minced prawns in place of minced meat.

Fried Water Spinach with Chilli Shrimp Paste Sauce (Kangkung Goreng Sambal Belacan)

300 g/10 oz water spinach (*kangkung*)
1 tbsp dried shrimps (*udang kering*)
3 shallots
2 red chillies
2 cm/¾" cube shrimp paste (*belacan*)
3 tbsp oil
2 tbsp water
salt to taste

- Wash and soak dried shrimps.
- Cut water spinach.
- Pound red chillies, shallots and shrimp paste. Spoon out.
- Strain dried shrimps and pound.
- Heat oil and fry chilli mixture till you get nice aroma.
- Add pounded dried shrimps and fry for a few minutes. Add water spinach and mix well.
- Add water and fry for one minute.
- Cover for one minute. Add salt. Taste and serve.

Variations
* Any one of the following vegetables can be used in place of water spinach: Chinese spinach (*bayam*), long beans, four angled beans, lady's fingers or watercress.
* You may use 150 g/5 oz prawns in place of dried shrimps.

VEGETABLES

Fried Angled Luffa Omelette

1 angled luffa (*ketola sanding*)
2 eggs
2 pips garlic
2 tbsp oil
1 tsp light soya sauce ⎫
¼ tsp salt ⎬ or to taste
⅛ tsp pepper ⎭

- Remove luffa skin. Cut angled luffa into 5 cm/2" lengths.
- Cut away centre seed section and shred about 3 mm/⅛" thick.
- Chop garlic.
- Beat eggs with light soya sauce.
- Heat oil and sauté garlic till golden brown.
- Add luffa and salt. Sauté till vegetable is soft.
- Pour beaten egg over luffa.
- Rotate wok to cover all the luffa and to get a round omelette. Lower fire.
- When egg is set and under-side is golden brown, cut into sections.
- Turn over each section and fry till golden brown. Dish out.
- Sprinkle with pepper and serve.

Variations

* If desired, add 90 g/3 oz prawns. When garlic is golden brown, sauté prawns before adding angled luffa.
* You may use 300 g/10 oz shredded head cabbage (*kubis*) in place of angled luffa.

Fried Diced Long Beans

4 long beans
1 piece hard bean curd (*taukua*)
1 small packet preserved radish (*lobak masin kering*)
150 g/4 oz prawns
2 tbsp peanuts
5 cm/2" carrot
2 red chillies
2 pips garlic
3 tbsp oil
¼ dsp salt ⎫
¼ tsp sugar ⎪
1 tsp light soya sauce ⎬ or to taste
⅛ tsp pepper ⎭

- Wash preserved radish and cut into smaller cubes.
- Season prawns with sugar and pepper.
- Dice long beans, hard bean curd and carrot.
- Shred chillies and chop garlic.
- Fry peanuts without oil over low fire until peanut skin can be removed easily. Cool and remove skin.
- Heat 1 tbsp oil and fry hard bean curd for two minutes. Dish out.
- Heat remaining oil and sauté garlic till golden brown.
- Add prawns and sauté for one minute.
- Add all the vegetables and hard bean curd except peanuts.
- Fry till vegetables are cooked.
- Add 1 tbsp water, salt, light soya sauce and pepper. Mix well. Taste.
- Garnish with peanuts and serve.

Variation

* You may use 1 tbsp dried shrimps (*udang kering*) in place of prawn.

VEGETABLES

Vegetable Curry

5 long beans
1 carrot
150 g/5 oz head cabbage (*kubis*)
2 brinjals/egg-plants/aubergines (*terung*)
2 tomatoes
½ grated coconut to get 70 ml/⅛ pt
thick coconut milk and 420 ml/¾ pt
thin coconut milk
8 shallots
2 red chillies or to taste
4 candlenuts (*buah keras*)
2½ cm/1" cube turmeric (*kunyit*)
2 tbsp oil
¼ tsp salt or to taste

- Cut long beans, head cabbage, carrot and brinjals.
- Soak brinjals.
- Slice three shallots.
- Pound finely remaining shallots, red chillies, candlenuts and turmeric.
- Heat oil. Sauté shallots till golden brown. Dish out.
- Add chilli mixture and sauté till there is nice aroma.
- Add all the vegetables, thin coconut milk and salt. Simmer for 10 minutes till vegetables are soft.
- Add thick coconut milk. Mix well. Taste.
- Garnish with fried shallots and serve.

Variation

* 150 g/5 oz prawns can also be added.

VEGETABLES

Grilled Brinjals

2 brinjals/egg-plants/aubergines (*terung*)
1 tbsp dried shrimps (*udang kering*)

For Sauce
2 pips garlic
2 shallots
1½ cm/½" cube shrimp paste (*belacan*)
2 red chillies
2 tbsp oil
sugar & pepper to taste
fried shallots

- Soak dried shrimps. Strain and pound. Remove from pounder.
- Pound finely chillies, shallots, garlic and shrimp paste.
- Wash brinjals and wipe dry. Do not remove skin.
- Heat grill. Grill brinjals for five to 10 minutes till soft.
- Remove brinjals skin and cut into suitable portions. Arrange on a plate.
- Heat 2 tbsp oil. Sauté chilli mixture till there is nice aroma.
- Add dried shrimps and sauté for two minutes.
- Add 2 tbsp water and fry till thick.
- Add sugar, salt and pepper to taste.
- Pour sauce over brinjals.
- Garnish with fried shallots.
- Serve hot.

Variations
* You may use 150 g/5 oz prawns in place of dried shrimps.
* Brinjals can be steamed instead of grilled.

Vegetable Cutlets

½ small yam bean/jicama (*sengkuang*)
1 small carrot
1 potato
1 onion
1 stalk spring onion
1 stalk Chinese celery
1 egg
2 tbsp bread crumbs
1 bowl oil for frying

- Boil potato and carrot till cooked. Remove skin from potato.
- Cut yam bean into small cubes. Chop onion, spring onion and Chinese celery separately.
- Beat egg with salt and pepper.
- Mash potato and carrot.
- Mix together all the vegetables and enough egg to make a dough.
- Roll into a sausage and cut into pieces of 2½ cm/1" in length.
- Coat with bread crumbs.
- Heat oil. Deep fry cutlets till golden brown.
- Serve with chilli sauce desired. Refer to section on Sauces.

VEGETARIAN DISHES

STUFFED HARD BEAN CURD **66**
(TAUKUA SUMBAT)

HARD BEAN CURD *SAMBAL* **66**
(SAMBAL TAUKUA)

FRIED FERMENTED SOYA BEAN **68**
(TEMPE GORENG)

FRIED HARD BEAN CURD WITH FERMENTED SOYA BEAN **68**
(TAUKUA GORENG DENGAN TEMPE)

LENTIL AND EGG CURRY **69**
(KARI DAL DAN TELUR)

BOILED VEGETABLES IN COCONUT MILK **70**
(MASAK LODEH)

FRIED MIXED VEGETABLES VEGETARIAN STYLE / CHYE CHOY **73**

HORSE GRAM CAKE **74**
(PAKODA)

SOFT BEAN CURD BALLS **74**

VEGETARIAN DISHES

Stuffed Hard Bean Curd
(Taukua Sumbat)

4 pieces hard bean curd (*taukua*)
4 tbsp oil
¼ yam bean/jicama (*sengkuang*)
5 cm/2" cucumber
2 tbsp beansprouts (*tauge*)

- Wash and wipe dry hard bean curd.
- Cut hard bean curd diagonally into two.
- Heat oil and fry hard bean curd till golden brown.
- Scald beansprouts.
- Shred yam beans and cucumber finely.
- Mix all the vegetables together.
- Make a slit at the diagonal edge of the hard bean curd.
- Remove some bean curd along the slit.
- Stuff vegetables in the slit.
- Serve hard bean curd with chilli sauce. Refer to section on Sauces.

Hard Bean Curd Sambal
(Sambal Taukua)

4 pieces hard bean curd (*taukua*)
6 shallots
2 sticks lemon grass (*serai*)
6 dried chillies
2 cm/¾" cube shrimp paste (*belacan*)
1 tsp tamarind paste (*asam jawa*)
6 - 8 tbsp water
½ tsp salt ⎫ or to
1 tsp sugar ⎭ taste
4 tbsp oil
1 onion
1 tomato

- Soak dried chillies and strain.
- Cut onion into rings. Cut tomato into wedges. Slice lemon grass.
- Mix tamarind paste with water and strain.
- Pound finely dried chillies together with lemon grass, shallots and shrimp paste.
- Wash and wipe dry hard bean curd. Cut diagonally into two.
- Heat oil and fry hard bean curd till golden brown on both sides. Dish out.
- Fry chilli mixture till there is nice aroma and oil appears.
- Add tamarind juice, salt, sugar and onion. When onion is soft, add tomato and hard bean curd. Simmer for a short while. Serve.

Variation

* Hard-boiled eggs or oily fish can be cooked using this method in place of hard bean curd.

VEGETARIAN DISHES

Fried Fermented Soya Bean
(Tempe Goreng)

2 packets fermented soya bean (*tempe*)
3 shallots
3 dried chillies
1 dsp vinegar
1 tsp sugar
½ tsp thick soya sauce
1 tsp thin soya sauce
1 dsp water
3 tbsp oil

- Wash and immediately wipe dry dried chillies. Cut coarsely.
- Slice shallots finely.
- Cut fermented soya bean into rectangular pieces.
- Heat oil and fry fermented soya bean till crispy. Dish out.
- Fry shallots till golden brown. Dish out.
- Fry dried chillies till crispy. Add in seasoning and fry for a short while. Taste.
- Add fermented soya bean pieces. Mix well. Serve.

Fried Hard Bean Curd with
Fermented Soya Bean
(Taukua Goreng dengan Tempe)

2 packets fermented soya bean (*tempe*)
2 pieces hard bean curd (*taukua*)
a few strands mungbean vermicelli/ sohoon
4 - 6 dried chillies
3 shallots
1 pip garlic
1½ cm/½" cube shrimp paste (*belacan*)
½ tsp salt ⎫ or to
½ tsp sugar ⎬ taste
1 tsp tamarind paste (*asam jawa*) ⎭
4 - 6 tbsp water
4 tbsp oil

- Soak dried chillies and mungbean vermicelli separately.
- Mix tamarind paste with water and strain.
- Cut hard bean curd and fermented soya bean into cubes.
- Pound together dried chillies, shallots, garlic and shrimp paste.
- Cut mungbean vermicelli into suitable lengths.
- Heat oil. Fry fermented soya bean till golden brown. Dish out.
- Fry hard bean curd till golden brown. Dish out.
- Leave 2 tbsp oil in pan/wok. Sauté chilli mixture till oil appears.
- Add in tamarind juice, salt and vinegar.
- When boiling, taste. Allow to simmer for a few minutes. Add the remaining ingredients.
- Simmer for a while. Serve.

VEGETARIAN DISHES

Lentil and Egg Curry
(Kari Dal dan Telur)

90 g/3 oz/3 tbsp lentils (*kacang dal*) – soak
for at least 4 hours
4 long beans
1 potato
1 tomato
1 brinjal/egg-plant/aubergine (*terung*)
4 shallots
2 pips garlic
2 slices ginger
1 sprig curry leaves
1 piece dried tamarind skin (*asam gelugur*)
½ grated coconut to get 70 ml/⅛ pt
thick coconut milk and 420 ml/¾ pt
thin coconut milk
1 tbsp curry powder
4 tbsp oil
¼ tsp salt or to taste
2 - 3 hard-boiled eggs

- Wash and strain lentils. Boil with 280 ml/
½ pt water and ½ tsp salt till soft. Strain.
- Cut hard-boiled eggs into half.
- Blend curry powder with a little thin
coconut milk to get a paste.
- Wash all vegetables and dried tamarind
skin.
- Wipe dry curry leaves.
- Cut potato into cubes and soak in water.
- Cut brinjal into wedges and soak in
water.
- Cut tomato into wedges.
- Cut long beans into short lengths.
- Shred ginger. Slice shallots and garlic.
- Heat oil. Fry shallots till golden brown.
Dish out.
- Sauté garlic, ginger and curry leaves.

- Add in curry paste. Fry till there is nice
aroma and oil appears.
- Add in lentils and fry lightly.
- Add in thin coconut milk, dried tamarind
skin and salt. Simmer for about 10 minutes.
- Add in potato, brinjal and long beans.
- When vegetables are nearly soft, add
tomato. Simmer for a while.
- Add in thick coconut milk and hard-boiled
eggs. When curry boils, taste and serve.

Variation

* This curry can be cooked without hard-
boiled eggs.

VEGETARIAN DISHES

Boiled Vegetables in Coconut Milk
(Masak Lodeh)

1 piece hard bean curd (*taukua*)
1 packet fermented soya bean (*tempe*)
1 piece dried bean curd skin (*fucuk*)
a few strands mungbean vermicelli/sohoon
2 large head cabbage leaves (*daun kubis*)
2 long beans
4 shallots
2 red chillies
1 stick lemon grass (*serai*)
½ grated coconut to get 70 ml/⅛ pt
thick coconut milk and
420 ml/¾ pt thin coconut milk
½ tsp salt
1 tbsp dried shrimps (*udang kering*)

- Soak mungbean vermicelli and dried shrimps separately. Drain.
- Pound dried shrimps.
- Cut hard bean curd into cubes.
- Cut head cabbage into square pieces.

- Cut long beans into suitable lengths. Slice shallots.
- Shred chillies. Bruise lemon grass.
- Cut fermented soya bean into rectangular pieces.
- Cut mungbean vermicelli into suitable lengths.
- Put thin coconut milk, all the vegetables, dried shrimps, fermented soya bean and salt in a pot.
- Boil and allow to simmer for five to 10 minutes till vegetables are almost soft.
- Wash dried bean curd skin and cut into big pieces. Add dried bean curd skin, hard bean curd cubes and mungbean vermicelli to simmer for a few minutes.
- When boiling add in thick coconut milk.
- Turn off fire. Remove lemon grass. Taste. Serve.

Variations
* Cook with 120 g/4 oz prawns instead of dried shrimps.
* Dried shrimps or prawns can also be left out from this dish.

VEGETARIAN DISHES

Fried Mixed Vegetables Vegetarian Style/Chye Choy

2 pieces hard bean curd (*taukua*)
6 fried bean curd balls/taw foo pok
(*tauhu bulat goreng*)
10 dried lily flowers/kamcam
2 pieces dried sweet bean curd sheets
(*timcuk*)
6 pieces black fungi/wan yee
2 large head cabbage leaves (*daun kubis*)
a few strands mungbean vermicelli/sohoon
1 tbsp soyabean paste (*taucu*)
1 red chilli
½ tsp salt or to taste
1 bowl oil

- Soak lily flowers and black fungi separately.
- Wipe dried sweet bean curd sheets and cut crosswise into strips. Do not wet it.
- Cut mungbean vermicelli into suitable lengths. Do not wet it.
- Wash and wipe dry hard bean curd. Dice.
- Cut fried bean curd balls into two.
- Remove stems from black fungi.

- Remove hard part from lily flowers and tie each into knot.
- Cut head cabbage leaves into squares.
- Shred chilli.
- Chop soyabean paste.
- Heat oil. Fry mungbean vermicelli quickly using low fire. When it expands and is still white in colour, dish out.
- Fry dried sweet bean curd strips for a short while. Dish out.
- Fry hard bean curd cubes. Dish out.
- Leave 3 tbsp oil in pan/wok. Sauté soyabean paste. Add lily flowers and black fungi. Fry for one minute. Add in 280 ml/½ pt water. When liquid boils simmer for five minutes.
- Add cabbage and salt. Stir to mix well.
- Add chilli, fried bean curd cubes, dried sweet bean curd strips, fried bean curd balls and mungbean vermicelli.
- Simmer for three minutes. If not enough gravy, add a little warm water. Taste and serve.

VEGETARIAN DISHES

Horse Gram Cake (Pakoda)

60 g/2 oz/2 tbsp skinless horse gram
powder/chick peas powder (*tepung
kacang kuda*)
¼ tsp salt or to taste
1 tsp curry powder
½ egg
¼ grated coconut to get 70 ml/⅛ pt
coconut milk
2 red chillies
1 sprig curry leaves
1 onion
1 tsp fennel (*jintan manis*)
1 bowl oil for deep frying

- Sift together flour, salt and curry powder.
- Make a well in the centre.
- Break in egg and add coconut milk.
- Mix thoroughly to get a thick batter.
- Allow to stand for 20 - 30 minutes.
- Chop red chillies and onion finely.
- Shred curry leaves finely.
- Add red chillies, curry leaves, onion and fennel to batter. Mix well.
- Heat oil. Drop batter spoon by spoon into oil and deep fry till golden brown.
- Dish out and drain oil.
- Serve with chilli sauce. Refer to section on Sauces.

Soft Bean Curd Balls

2 pieces soft bean curd (*tauhu*)
90 g/3 oz prawns
¼ tsp sugar
¼ tsp pepper
¼ yam bean/jicama (*sengkuang*)
1 egg
1 tbsp cornflour
¼ tsp salt
1 bowl oil for deep frying

- Dice finely prawns and yam bean.
- Season prawns with sugar and pepper.
- Beat egg. Mash soft bean curd.
- Mix together soft bean curd, egg, prawns, yam bean, cornflour and salt.
- Heat oil. Shape soft bean curd mixture into balls.
- Put into oil and deep fry till golden brown.
- Dish out and drain.
- Serve with chilli sauce. Refer to section on Sauces.

Variations

* Season prawns with 1 tsp sesame oil and 1 tsp light soya sauce.
* Add 1 tsp curry powder to soft bean curd mixture.
* Serve soft bean curd balls with sweet and sour sauce. Refer to section on Sauces.
* Serve soft bean curd balls with salad. Refer to section on Salad.
* Use dried shrimps instead of fresh prawns.
* Soft bean curd balls can be cooked without prawns.

EGGS

BAKED SWEET EGG CUSTARD **76**

STEAMED SAVOURY EGG CUSTARD **76**

EGG OMELETTE **78**

FRIED OMELETTE WITH LONG BEANS **78**

MINI OMELETTE WITH MINCED MEAT **78**

EGG *SAMBAL* **80**

EGG CURRY **80**

EGGS

Baked Sweet Egg Custard

4 eggs
420 ml/¾ pt milk
4 tbsp sugar or to taste
½ tsp vanilla essence

- Heat oven at 350°F/180°C/4.
- Grease pyrex bowl.
- Beat eggs with milk, sugar and vanilla essence till sugar dissolves. Strain.
- Pour egg mixture into the bowl and stand bowl in the middle of a tray containing water.
- Bake for 40 minutes till cooked. Serve hot.

Variation

* Sweet Egg Custard can also be steamed for 15-20 minutes. Cover bowl with grease proof paper before steaming. This egg custard can also be used as filling for egg tart.

Steamed Savoury Egg Custard

4 eggs
1 dsp light soya sauce
280 ml/½ pt cool boiled water
salt & pepper to taste
1 stalk spring onions

- Beat eggs with water, salt and pepper.
- Pour egg mixture into a bowl.
- Cover bowl with grease proof paper.
- Steam for 10 - 15 minutes.
- Dice spring onions.
- Sprinkle light soya sauce, pepper and spring onions on top of egg castard. Serve hot.

Variations

* One of the following ingredients can be added:

(a) 90 g/3 oz chopped fresh prawns and a few strands of soaked mungbean vermicelli/sohoon. Cut into 10 cm/4" long.
(b) 1 tbsp pounded dried shrimps.
(c) 90 g/3 oz chopped meat.
(d) 90 g/3 oz fish meat diced into small pieces.
(e) 90 g/3 oz diced fried fish paste. For making fish paste, refer to recipe of Fish Paste in Fish section.

EGGS

Egg Omelette

2 eggs
½ medium-sized onion
2 tbsp oil
salt and pepper to taste

- Beat eggs with salt and pepper.
- Dice onion.
- Heat oil in wok.
- Add in onion and fry till soft.
- Pour in egg mixture. Rotate wok to get a round omelette.
- When the under-side of mixture becomes golden brown, fold it into half.
- Serve immediately.

N.B. Besides onion, the following ingredients can be added.
(a) 90 g/3 oz fresh prawns diced and 2 red chillies chopped coarsely. Fry prawns and chillies before adding egg mixture.
(b) 30 g/1 oz grated cheese, 1 small tomato diced and 1 red chilli chopped coarsely.

Fried Omelette with Long Beans

4 eggs
90 g/3 oz prawns
150 g/5 oz long beans
1 stalk spring onion
2 red chillies
2 shallots
2 pips garlic
2 tbsp oil
salt, sugar & pepper to taste

- Season prawns with a little salt and sugar.
- Beat eggs with salt and pepper.
- Dice long beans and spring onions.
- Shred chillies.
- Slice shallots and chop garlic.
- Heat oil in wok. Add in shallots and garlic. Fry till golden brown.
- Add in prawns and fry for one minute.
- Add in long beans and fry for two minutes.
- Add in salt to taste.
- Add in egg mixture. Rotate wok to get a round omelette.
- When omelette thickens, sprinkle spring onions, chillies and pepper on top.
- Roll in a sausage and cut into smaller portions. Serve.

Mini Omelette with Minced Meat

4 eggs
150 g/5 oz minced meat
1 small onion
3 tbsp oil
salt and pepper to taste

- Chop onion.
- Heat 1 tbsp oil in wok. Fry onion lightly. Add in minced meat and fry for one minute. Turn off fire.
- Beat eggs with minced meat, onion, salt and pepper.
- Heat oil in wok.
- Pour in one ladle of egg mixture.
- When the mixture thickens and under-side becomes golden brown, fold it into half.
- Repeat the above process until all the egg mixture is finished. Serve.

Variation

* 150 g/5 oz fresh prawns can be used in place of minced meat. Cut prawns into smaller pieces.

EGGS

Egg Sambal

3 hard-boiled eggs
4 dried chillies or to taste
4 shallots
1½ cm/½" cube shrimp paste (*belacan*)
1 tsp tamarind paste (*asam jawa*)
or to taste
2 tbsp oil
salt & pepper to taste

- Soak dried chillies.
- Cut hard-boiled eggs into halves.
- Mix tamarind paste with 3 - 4 tbsp water. Strain to get tamarind juice.
- Pound dried chillies with shallots and shrimp paste.
- Heat oil in wok. Add in chilli mixture and a little salt. Lower fire. Fry till you get nice aroma.
- Add in tamarind juice and a little sugar.
- Cook till it thickens. Taste.
- Add in eggs and simmer for one minute. Serve.

Variations

* One of the following ingredients can be used in place of hard-boiled eggs:
(a) 3 egg omelettes.
(b) 90 g/3 oz prawns.

Egg Curry

3 hard-boiled eggs
4 shallots
1 tbsp curry powder
½ grated coconut to get 420 ml/¾ pt coconut milk
2 tbsp oil
salt to taste

- Cut hard-boiled eggs into halves.
- Slice shallots.
- Mix curry powder with a little coconut milk to make a paste.
- Heat oil in wok. Add in shallots and fry till golden brown.
- Add in curry paste. Lower fire and fry till oil appears.
- Add in coconut milk and salt. Simmer for three to four minutes. Taste.
- Add in eggs and simmer for one minute. Serve.

Variations

* You may use 120 g/4 oz fresh prawns or 90 g/3 oz fish or fish balls in place of hard-boiled eggs.

FISH

STEAMED FISH 82

FRIED FISH 82

SOUR SALTED FISH 82

FISH CURRY 83

FISH MOOLI 83

GRILLED STUFFED FISH 84

SWEET AND SOUR FISH 84

FISH BALL SOUP 86

FISH PASTE 86

STUFFED SOFT BEAN CURD WITH FISH PASTE 89
(YONG TAUHU)

EGG AND FISH ROLL 89

MALAYSIAN FISH CUSTARD 91
(OTAK-OTAK)

ANCHOVY *SAMBAL* 91
(SAMBAL IKAN BILIS)

ANCHOVY SAMBAL WITH *BELIMBING* FRUITS 92
(SAMBAL IKAN BILIS DENGAN BUAH BELIMBING BESI)

FRIED PRAWNS WITH TAMARIND PASTE 92
(UDANG ASAM GORENG)

PRAWN FRITTERS 94

DRIED SHRIMP *SAMBAL* 94

FISH

Steamed Fish

300 g/10 oz fish
1½ cm/½" ginger
2 pips garlic
2 tbsp oil
1 tbsp light soya sauce
1 stalk spring onion

- Shred ginger. Chop garlic finely. Dice spring onion finely.
- Mix ginger and garlic with oil.
- Stuff inside of fish with some ginger mixture and spread remaining mixture on fish.
- Steam for 10 - 15 minutes till cooked. Sprinkle light soya sauce on fish.
- Garnish with spring onion and pepper. Serve hot.

Fried Fish

300 g/10 oz fish
1 tsp turmeric powder or curry powder
½ tsp salt or to taste
6 tbsp oil

- Cut fish into pieces if desired. Season fish with salt.
- Rinse and wipe dry the fish. Rub turmeric powder or curry powder on the inside and all over the fish.
- Leave for at least 15 minutes.
- Heat oil. Fry fish till both sides are golden brown. Make sure that oil is hot before putting in fish so that it will not stick. You may lower fire later. Serve hot.

Sour Salted Fish

90 g/3 oz salted fish
2 tsp tamarind paste (*asam jawa*) } or to taste
1 tsp sugar
1 onion
2 long beans
2 pips garlic
4 shallots
1 green chilli
1 red chilli
2 tbsp oil

- Cut salted fish into thin slices.
- Mix tamarind paste with 140 ml/¼ pt water and strain.
- Slice shallots and garlic. Cut onion into rings.
- Cut long beans into suitable lengths.
- Cut chillies into halves lengthwise and cut diagonally into smaller pieces.
- Heat oil, fry shallots till golden brown. Dish out.
- Fry salted fish till you get nice aroma. Dish out.
- Sauté garlic till golden brown. Add onion rings and fry lightly.
- Add salted fish, tamarind juice and sugar. Simmer for a few minutes.
- Add long beans and chillies.
- Simmer till vegetables are cooked. Taste.
- Garnish with fried shallots before serving.

FISH

Fish Curry

300 g/10 oz oily fish
4 lady's fingers
1 tomato
½ grated coconut to get 70 ml/⅛ pt
thick coconut milk and 420 ml/¾ pt
thin coconut milk
6 shallots
2 pips garlic
1 sprig curry leaf – optional
1 tbsp curry powder
1 dsp tamarind paste (*asam jawa*)
½ tsp salt or to taste
3 tbsp oil

- Cut fish into pieces if desired. Season with salt.
- Blend curry powder with 3 tbsp thin coconut milk to a paste.
- Mix tamarind paste with 6 tbsp thin coconut milk and strain.
- Wipe dry curry leaves. Cut lady's fingers into suitable lengths.
- Cut tomato into wedges.
- Slice garlic and shallots.
- Heat oil. Fry ½ quantity of shallots till golden brown. Dish out.
- Fry remaining shallots, garlic and curry leaves till you get nice aroma.
- Add in tamarind juice and salt. Lower fire. Simmer for a while.
- Add thin coconut milk. Simmer.
- Add lady's fingers, tomato and fish. Simmer till fish and vegetables are cooked. Add thick coconut milk.
- When curry begins to simmer, turn off fire. Garnish with fried shallots before serving.

Variations
* Cook with prawns instead of fish.
* Cook with brinjal/egg-plant/aubergine instead of lady's fingers.

Fish Mooli

300 g/10 oz fish
½ grated coconut to get 70 ml/⅛ pt
thick coconut milk and 210 ml/⅜ pt
thin coconut milk
1 red chilli
1 green chilli
4 slices ginger
8 shallots
2 pips garlic
1 stick lemon grass (*serai*)
1 onion
2 tbsp oil
½ tsp salt or to taste
½ tsp turmeric powder (*serbuk kunyit*)
juice of 1 lime if desired

- Cut fish into pieces if desired.
- Season with salt.
- Slice shallots and garlic.
- Shred ginger and chillies.
- Bruise lemon grass.
- Cut onion into rings.
- Heat oil. Fry ½ quantity of shallots till golden brown. Dish out.
- Fry garlic, ginger, onion, turmeric powder and remaining shallots.
- Add thin coconut milk, chillies and salt.
- Simmer for about five minutes. Add fish.
- When fish is cooked, add thick coconut milk. Turn off fire. Taste. Add lime juice if desired. Garnish with fried shallots before serving.

FISH

Grilled Stuffed Fish

300 g/10 oz horse mackerals (*cencaru*)
4 shallots
1 pip garlic
4 dried chillies
1 candle nut (*buah keras*)
1½ cm/½" cube shrimp paste (*belacan*)
1 stick lemon grass (*serai*)
1 slice ginger
1 tsp tamarind paste (*asam jawa*)
½ tsp sugar or to taste
¼ tsp salt
1 tbsp oil
banana leaf measuring 25 cm/10" square –
softened

- Soak dried chillies in hot water.
- Slit fish along both sides of the fins. Season with salt.
- Mix 2 tbsp water with tamarind paste. Strain.
- Slice lemon grass.
- Pound dried chillies, shallots, garlic, candlenut, lemon grass, ginger and shrimp paste.
- Heat oil. Fry chilli mixture till you get nice aroma and oil appears.
- Add tamarind juice, sugar and salt. Simmer till almost dry. Taste.
- Stuff fish with fried mixture along the slit.
- Wrap fish in greased banana leaf. Grill both sides of fish for 20 - 30 minutes till cooked.
- Remove banana leaf and serve hot.

Variation

* Deep fry the fish without wrapping it in banana leaf. Remove the hard skin before serving.

Sweet and Sour Fish

300 g/10 oz fish
1 dsp cornflour
6 tbsp oil

For Sauce

2 tbsp tomato sauce
1 tbsp chilli sauce – optional
1 dsp vinegar or lime juice   } mixed
1 tsp light soya sauce   together
1 tsp sugar
⅛ tsp pepper
½ tsp cornflour   } mixed
4 - 6 tbsp water   together
2 pips garlic
1 slice ginger

- Season fish with salt for about five minutes.
- Wash and wipe dry fish.
- Chop garlic finely. Shred ginger finely.
- Heat oil. Coat fish lightly with 1 dsp cornflour and fry till both sides are golden brown. Make sure that oil is hot before putting in fish. Lower fire later. Dish fish into serving plate.
- Leave 1 dsp oil in wok.
- Fry garlic and ginger till golden brown.
- Add in sauce mixture and mix well. Add in enough cornflour mixture. Stir all the time.
- Simmer and taste.
- Spoon sauce onto fish. Garnish and serve hot.

Suggested Garnishes

* Tomato, cucumber, red chilli and spring onion.
* Pickled papaya – refer to recipe of Pickled Papaya, section on Preserves.
* Tomato, cucumber and stewed pineapple.

FISH

Fish Ball Soup

Fish Paste

150 g/5 oz Spanish mackerals or herrings
(*tenggiri atau parang*)
¼ tsp salt or to taste
1 - 1½ tsp water
1 dsp oil

Basic Anchovy Stock

1 rice bowl anchovies (*ikan bilis*)
3 - 4 slices ginger
1 tbsp oil
840 ml/1½ pt water

Other Ingredients

a few strands mungbean vermicelli/
sohoon
2 slices ginger
2 head cabbage leaves (*daun kubis*)
½ carrot
½ tsp salt to taste
½ tsp pepper
2 tbsp oil

- Prepare fish paste following method in recipe of Fish Paste in this section.
- Prepare stock following method in recipe of Basic Anchovy Stock in section on Soups.
- Cut mungbean vermicelli into suitable lengths and soak.
- Slice carrot and cut cabbage.
- Dip hand in salt water and shape fish balls.
- Put fish balls in boiling stock.
- When they float, add vegetables and simmer till vegetables are cooked.
- Add mungbean vermicelli. Add salt and taste. Sprinkle pepper and serve hot.

Variation

* Use Chinese flowering cabbage/mustard leaves (*sawi*) instead of head cabbage (*kubis*).

Fish Paste

150 g/5 oz Spanish mackerals or herrings
(*tenggiri atau parang*)
¼ tsp salt or to taste
1 - 1½ dsp water
1 dsp oil

- Scrape fish from skin and bones.
- Add salt. Mix well.
- Use a clean, dry chopping board, chop fish with the back of the cleaver until fish becomes a smooth moist paste. Add a little water whenever the fish meat becomes too sticky.
- Put fish paste into a bowl.
- Add in oil and mix thoroughly to get a smooth texture. Use as desired.

FISH

(i) Fillet fish.

ii) Separate fish meat from skin. Chop fish meat until it becomes a smooth paste.

FISH

Stuffed Soft Bean Curd with Fish Paste (Yong Tauhu)

Fish Paste
150 g/5 oz Spanish mackerals or herrings
(*tenggiri atau parang*)
¼ tsp salt or to taste
1 - 1½ dsp water
1 dsp oil

Other Ingredients
6 pieces soft soya bean curd (*tauhu*)
6 tbsp oil

Soyabean Paste Sauce (Sos Taucu)
1 tbsp soyabean paste (taucu)
1 pip garlic
⅛ tsp pepper or to taste
1 tsp sugar
½ tsp cornflour
4 tbsp water
} mix together

- Prepare fish paste following method in recipe of Fish Paste in this section.
- Wipe dry soft bean curd and cut into halves diagonally.
- Slit diagonal side and remove enough bean curd to stuff fish paste. Fill up with fish paste.
- Chop finely garlic and soyabean paste separately.
- Heat oil. Fry bean curd on all sides till golden brown.
- Leave 1 dsp oil and fry garlic till golden brown. Add soyabean paste and fry for a while.
- Add water and cornflour mixture and simmer for two minutes. Add more water if sauce is too thick. Taste.
- Serve bean curd with sauce.

Variations
* Steam bean curd instead of frying.
* Stuffed bean curd can also be served with the following sauces: sweet sour sauce, instant chilli sauce or chilli garlic sauce.
* Chillies, brinjal/egg-plant/aubergine, lady's fingers and bitter gourd can also be stuffed with fish paste.

Egg and Fish Roll

Fish Paste
150 g/ 5 oz Spanish mackerals or herrings
(*tenggiri atau parang*)
¼ tsp salt or to taste
1 - 1½ dsp water
1 dsp oil

Egg Omelette
2 eggs
2 tbsp water
¼ tsp salt
⅛ tsp pepper
} or to taste
2 tsp oil

- Prepare fish paste. Refer to method in recipe of Fish Paste in this section.
- Beat eggs with water, salt and pepper. Heat oil and make one or two omelettes.
- Spread fish paste on omelette till 1½ cm/ ½ " from side of omelette.
- Roll up neatly.
- Steam for 10 - 15 minutes until fish is cooked.
- Cut fish roll into slices.
- Serve with sauce separately or pour on top.
- Choose one of these sauces in section on Sauces – Instant Chilli Sauce, Sweet and Sour Sauce or Soyabean Paste Sauce.

FISH

Malaysian Fish Custard (Otak-otak)

150 g/5 oz fish
1 tsp curry powder ⎱ or to
¼ tsp salt ⎰ taste
2 eggs
¾ grated coconut to get 280 ml/½ pt
coconut milk
1 sprig annatto leaves (*daun kesum*) –
optional
5 dried chillies
1 stick lemon grass (*serai*)
2 candlenuts (*buah keras*)
1½ cm/½" turmeric (*kunyit*)
1½ cm/½" galangal (*lengkuas*)
4 shallots
2 pips garlic
1½ cm/½" cube shrimp paste (*belacan*)

- Soak dried chillies.
- Cut fish into thin slices. Season with curry powder and salt.
- Fry 2 tbsp grated coconut without oil over low fire, stirring all the time till golden brown.
- Pound fried grated coconut immediately to a fine powder or use desiccated coconut.
- Chop finely annatto leaves if used.
- Slice lemon grass.
- Pound finely chillies, lemon grass, turmeric, candlenuts and shrimp paste.
- Beat eggs and salt.
- Mix together all the ingredients evenly.
- Pour into a pyrex dish and steam for 20 minutes till cooked.

Variation
* Bake instead of steam.

Anchovy Sambal (Sambal Ikan Bilis)

90 g/3 oz anchovies (*ikan bilis*)
1 onion
10 dried chillies
10 shallots
2 sticks lemon grass (*serai*)
3¾ cm/1½" cube shrimp paste (*belacan*)
6 tbsp oil
1 tbsp tamarind paste (*asam jawa*)
¼ tsp salt ⎱ or to
1 tsp sugar ⎰ taste

- Soak dried chillies.
- Wash and wipe dry anchovies.
- Mix tamarind paste with 6 - 8 tbsp water. Strain.
- Slice onion into rings.
- Slice lemon grass.
- Pound chillies, lemon grass, shallots and shrimp paste.
- Heat oil and fry anchovies over low fire, stirring all the time till golden brown. Dish out.
- Fry chilli mixture till there is nice aroma and oil appears.
- Add in onion and stir. Add tamarind juice, sugar and salt. Simmer for about five minutes.
- Add anchovies. Stir well. Taste. Serve.

FISH

Anchovy Sambal with Belimbing Fruits (Sambal Ikan Bilis dengan Buah Belimbing Besi)

90 g/3 oz anchovies (*ikan bilis*)
10 *belimbing* fruits (*belimbing besi*)
½ grated coconut to get 280 ml/½ pt coconut milk
1 onion
10 dried chillies
8 shallots
2 cm/¾" cube shrimp paste (*belacan*)
2 sticks lemon grass (*serai*)
½ tsp salt ⎫
1 tsp sugar ⎬ or to taste
3 tbsp oil ⎭

- Soak dried chillies.
- Wash and strain anchovies.
- Slice onion into rings.
- Slice lemon grass.
- Cut *belimbing* fruits diagonally into suitable sizes.
- Pound chillies, lemon grass, shallots and shrimp paste.
- Heat oil. Fry pounded mixture till you get nice aroma and oil appears. Add onion rings. Fry lightly. Add in coconut milk and salt.
- Simmer for three minutes.
- Add anchovies and *belimbing* fruits. Simmer till anchovies and *belimbing* fruits are soft.
- Add sugar and salt. Taste.

Variation
* Use tomatoes instead of *belimbing* fruits.

Fried Prawns with Tamarind Paste (Udang Asam Goreng)

300 g/10 oz medium-sized prawns
1½ tbsp tamarind paste (*asam jawa*)
4 tbsp water
¼ tsp salt
1 rice bowl oil

- Mix tamarind paste with water.
- Cut off sharp ends from prawns but leave shell intact.
- Wash and drain prawns.
- Season prawns with tamarind paste and salt for ½ an hour.
- Cook prawn mixture till almost dry. Remove tamarind seeds.
- Heat oil. Fry prawns till shells are crisp using low fire. Keep stirring to avoid prawns from sticking to wok.
- Serve hot.

Variation
* Fish can be cooked using this recipe.

Suggestions for Serving
* Fried prawns with tamarind paste can be served with coconut milk rice (*nasi lemak*) and chilli shrimp paste sauce (*sambal belacan*). Refer to section on One-dish Meal.

FISH

Prawn Fritters

300 g/10 oz medium-sized prawns
½ tsp sugar
⅛ tsp pepper

For Batter

2 tbsp dry rice flour (*tepung beras*)
⅛ tsp salt
¼ tsp curry powder if desired
4 - 6 tbsp water
⅛ tsp slake lime (*kapur*)
1 large bowl oil for deep frying

- Shell prawns leaving tails intact.
- Slit back of prawns to remove veins. Season with sugar and pepper.
- Sift together rice flour, salt and curry powder. Mix to a thick consistency with water.
- Heat oil. Add slake lime to batter. Mix well.
- Dip prawns in batter and deep fry till golden brown.
- Serve with chilli sauce desired. Refer to section on Sauces.

Variations

* Slices of fish or meat can be cooked using this method.
* Other recipes on thick batter can also be used. Refer to section on Batter.

Dried Shrimp Sambal

4 tbsp dried shrimps (*udang kering*)
10 shallots
3 sticks lemon grass (*serai*)
8 - 10 dried chillies
2½ cm/1" cube shrimp paste (*belacan*)
1 dsp tamarind paste (*asam jawa*)
4 tbsp water
¼ tsp salt
1 tsp sugar　} or to taste
4 tbsp oil

- Soak dried chillies and dried shrimps separately. Strain.
- Slice lemon grass.
- Mix tamarind paste with water and strain.
- Pound dried shrimps and keep aside.
- Pound finely dried chillies, lemon grass, shallots and shrimp paste. Fry chilli mixture till there is nice aroma and oil appears.
- Add in dried shrimps. Fry lightly. Add in tamarind juice, sugar and salt. Mix well.
- Simmer till almost dry or dry as desired using low fire and stirring all the time.

MEAT

STEAMED MINCED MEAT **96**

STEAMED MEAT WITH SHRIMP PASTE **96**
(DAGING KUKUS BELACAN)

FRIED MEAT BALLS **97**

BURGER **97**

MEAT STEW **98**

CHICKEN CURRY **98**

FRIED SPICY MEAT **99**
(DAGING GORENG BEREMPAH)

MEAT *RENDANG*/SPICY MEAT IN COCONUT MILK **100**
(RENDANG DAGING)

GRILLED *PANDAN* CHICKEN **102**
(AYAM PANGGANG DAUN PANDAN)

MEAT

Steamed Minced Meat

120 g/4 oz minced meat
3 tsp light soya sauce or to taste
¼ tsp pepper
1 dsp oil
½ tsp cornflour
2 tbsp water

- Add oil, 2 tsp light soya sauce, pepper and cornflour to minced meat.
- Mix well.
- Put seasoned meat into a suitable-sized plate and press meat lightly to get an even surface.
- Mix together remaining light soya sauce and water.
- Pour mixture onto meat.
- Steam meat for 10-15 minutes till cooked. Serve.

Steamed Meat with Shrimp Paste (Daging Kukus Belacan)

120 g/4 oz meat
2 cm/¾" cube shrimp paste (*belacan*)
2 shallots
1 pip garlic
1 slice ginger
1 red chilli
1 green chilli
¼ tsp sugar
pinch of salt
juice of 1 lime
1 tbsp oil

} or to taste

- Slice meat thinly.
- Add oil to meat. Mix together.
- Slice shallots lengthwise.
- Slice chillies and garlic finely.
- Shred ginger.
- Dissolve shrimp paste with 1½ tbsp water.
- Mix together meat, vegetables, shrimp paste mixture, sugar and salt. Put to steam for 10 - 15 minutes till cooked.
- Add enough lime juice. Taste and serve.

MEAT

Fried Meat Balls

120 g/4 oz minced meat
½ - 1 egg
¼ tsp salt ⎫ to
¼ tsp pepper ⎬ season
1 potato ⎭ meat
1 onion
1 tbsp peas
2 pips garlic
½ tsp thick soya sauce ⎫
1 dsp thin soya sauce ⎪
¼ tsp sugar ⎬ mix
⅛ tsp pepper ⎪ together
½ tsp cornflour ⎭
4 - 6 tbsp water
1 large bowl oil for deep fat frying

- Season meat with salt and pepper.
- Add ¼ tsp cornflour and enough beaten egg to get a moist, firm mixture.
- Shape into balls.
- Cut potato into strips. Soak in water.
- Slice onion.
- Chop finely garlic.
- Heat oil. Wipe dry potato strips. Deep fry potato strips till golden brown.
- Deep fry meat balls till golden brown.
- Leave 1 dsp oil in pan/wok. Sauté garlic till golden brown. Add onions. Sauté again. Add sauce mixture. Stir well.
- When liquid simmers add meat balls, peas and potato strips. Stir well. Dish out.

Variations

* Serve fried meat balls with sweet and sour sauce or barbecue sauce. Refer to section on Sauces.

* Serve fried meat balls with pickles or salad. Refer to section on Preserves or Salad.

Burger

150 g/5 oz minced meat
1 onion
2 pips garlic
⅛ tsp pepper ⎫
¼ tsp salt ⎪ or to
1 tsp light soya sauce ⎬ taste
1 tsp cornflour ⎭
3 tbsp oil or 1 tbsp margarine or butter

- Chop finely onion and garlic.
- Mix all the ingredients together evenly to get a firm mixture.
- Divide mixture into four to six portions.
- Shape each portion into flat rounds of about 1½ cm/½" thick.
- Heat oil or margarine.
- Fry burger on both sides till golden brown.
- Sandwich burger in between buns or toasted bread.
- Serve with sauce of choice, salad or pickles. Refer to section on Sauces, Salad or Preserves.

MEAT

Meat Stew

300 g/10 oz meat
1 tbsp light soya sauce
¼ tsp pepper
1 tsp cornflour
2½ cm/1" cinnamon (*kayu manis*)
1 carrot
1 onion
1 potato
2 tbsp peas
2 tbsp oil
¼ tsp thick soya sauce – optional
½ tsp salt

- Cut meat into suitable-sized pieces.
- Season meat with light soya sauce, pepper and ½ tsp cornflour.
- Heat 2 tbsp oil. Fry cinnamon till you get nice aroma.
- Add meat. Sauté for a short while.
- Add 420 ml/¾ pt water. Stir to mix ingredients.
- When water boils, lower fire and simmer for 20 - 30 minutes.
- Cut onion into wedges.
- Cut carrot and potato into cubes. Soak potato in water.
- When meat is almost cooked, add vegetables. Continue to simmer until the vegetables and meat are cooked. Add peas.
- Blend remaining cornflour with 1 tbsp water and thick soya sauce, if used. Pour into simmering mixture and stir to mix well.
- Add salt. Taste. Serve.

Chicken Curry

½ chicken
1 tbsp curry powder
½ grated coconut to get 70 ml/⅛ pt thick coconut milk and 560 ml/1 pt thin coconut milk
6 shallots
2 pips garlic
1 stick lemon grass (*serai*)
2 candlenuts (*buah keras*)
2½ cm/1" cinnamon (*kayu manis*)
2 chillies
1 potato
½ tsp salt
4 tbsp water

- Slice shallots, garlic and lemon grass.
- Cut chicken and potato into suitable-sized pieces. Soak potato.
- Pound finely chillies together with lemon grass, candlenuts, shallots and garlic.
- Blend curry powder into a paste with 2 - 3 tbsp thin coconut milk.
- Heat oil. Fry cinnamon until you get nice aroma. Add chilli mixture and salt. Use low fire. Fry till there is nice aroma.
- Add curry paste. Fry till oil appears.
- Add chicken. Use bigger fire. Stir well. Fry for one minute.
- Add thin coconut milk. Mix well.
- When boiling, lower fire and allow to simmer till chicken is nearly cooked.
- Add potato. When boiling again simmer till chicken and potato are cooked.
- Add thick coconut milk. Mix well.
- When mixture starts boiling turn off fire.
- Taste and serve.

MEAT

Fried Spicy Meat
(Daging Goreng Berempah)

300 g/10 oz meat
¾ grated coconut to get 280 ml/½ pt
coconut milk
1 tsp lime juice
2 tbsp oil
1 tsp coriander (*ketumbar*)
1 tsp fennel (*jintan manis*)
1 tsp cumin (*jintan putih*)
1 stick lemon grass (*serai*)
1½ cm/½" cube dry turmeric
(*kunyit kering*)
6 - 8 dried chillies
2 slices galangal (*lengkuas*)
¼ tsp salt

- Soak dried chillies.
- Slice lemon grass. Shred galangal.
- Pound coriander, fennel, cumin, lemon grass, dry turmeric, galangal and dried chillies.
- Cut meat into bite size pieces. Or slice meat crosswise.
- Season meat with pounded ingredients, coconut milk, salt and lime juice for at least ½ an hour.
- Heat oil. Fry meat.
- Allow to simmer for 15 - 20 minutes till meat is cooked.
- Make sure the fire is not high. Stir often to avoid meat from sticking to pan/wok.
- If drier meat is preferred, then allow it to simmer longer.
- Dish out onto a pyrex dish. Grill meat for a short while before serving.

Variation

* After seasoning skewer the meat. Then put to grill. Serve with sauce desired. Refer to section on Sauces.

MEAT

Meat Rendang/Spicy Meat in Coconut Milk (Rendang Daging)

300 g/10 oz meat – beef or mutton
1 grated coconut to get 1 litre/1¾ pt
coconut milk
8 - 10 dried chillies
8 shallots
2 pips garlic
2 sticks lemon grass (*serai*)
1 slice ginger 1½ cm/½" thick
1 turmeric leaf (*daun kunyit*)
1 cm/⅜" cube turmeric (*kunyit*)
1 slice galangal (*lengkuas*)
2 pieces dried tamarind skins
(*asam gelugur*)
½ tsp salt or to taste

- Soak chillies. Drain and pound finely.
- Slice meat crosswise.
- Slice shallots, garlic and lemon grass.
- Shred ginger, turmeric leaf and galangal.
- Put coconut milk into pan/wok.
- Add all the other ingredients except dried tamarind skins.
- Put to boil. Lower fire and allow to simmer for 15 - 20 minutes before adding dried tamarind skins.
- Stir occasionally to prevent mixture from sticking to wok.
- Continue to simmer mixture. Stir more regularly till   meat is soft and mixture is almost dry. Taste and serve.

Variation
* Use chicken but add pieces of chicken only after simmering coconut milk and other ingredients for 15 minutes.

MEAT

Grilled Pandan Chicken
(Ayam Panggang Daun Pandan)

½ chicken
8 - 10 large screwpine leaves/
pandan leaves
½ grated coconut to get 70 - 140 ml/
⅛ - ¼ pt thick coconut milk
1½ cm/½" galangal (*lengkuas*)
¼ tsp pepper
¼ tsp coriander powder (*serbuk ketumbar*)
¼ tsp fennel (*jintan manis*)
½ tsp sugar } or to
¼ tsp salt } taste

- Pound galangal to get its juice.
- Mix all the ingredients together except chicken and screwpine leaves.

- Cut chicken into 8 - 10 suitable-sized pieces.
- Marinate chicken with coconut milk mixture for at least ½ an hour.
- Wash and wipe dry screwpine leaves.
- Wrap each piece of chicken with a screwpine leaf and staple the ends.
- Grill both sides of wrapped chicken for 15 - 20 minutes till chicken is cooked.
- Remove screwpine leaves or serve chicken wrapped in them.

Variations
* Deep fry wrapped chicken.
* Wrap chicken with grease proof paper and deep fry the packets.

DRINKS

BASIC SYRUP 104

PAPAYA DRINK 104

LIME DRINK 105

PINEAPPLE DRINK 105

SYRUP MILK DRINK 106
(AIR BANDUNG)

SOYABEAN MILK 106

AGAR DRINK 106
(MINUMAN AGAR-AGAR)

EGG TEA   108

EGG FLIP 108

CREAM STYLE CORN DRINK 108

BARLEY WATER 108

DRINKS

Basic Syrup

90 g/3 oz/3 tbsp sugar
140 ml/¼ pt water

First Method

- Boil sugar and water till sugar dissolves.
- Cool before use.

Second Method

- Put sugar into a bowl.
- Pour freshly boiled water over it.
- Stir till sugar dissolves.
- Cool before use.

Variation

* For first method, 2 knotted screwpine leaves/*pandan* leaves can be added.

Papaya Drink

240 g/8 oz ripe papaya
560 ml/1 pt cold water
90 g/3 oz/3 tbsp sugar
140 ml/¼ pt boiled water

- Put sugar into a bowl. Pour freshly boiled water over it. Stir till sugar dissolves. Cool.
- Cut papaya into big cubes.
- Place papaya on aluminium sieve on a bowl.
- Pass papaya through sieve with a wooden spoon.
- Pour papaya juice and syrup into a glass jug.
- Add enough cold water to taste and mix well.
- Cool in refrigerator before serving.

Variations

* You may use 280 ml/½ pt milk and 280 ml/½ pt cold water in place of 560 ml/1 pt cold water.
* 480 g/1 lb water melon may be used in place of papaya.

DRINKS

Lime Drink

3 - 4 limes
840 ml/1½ pt cold water
90 g/3 oz/3 tbsp sugar
140 ml/¼ pt boiled water

- Wash and wipe dry limes. Roll each lime on table with palm to soften it.
- Cut lime skin as thinly as possible. Do not cut the white part because it will make the drink bitter.
- Pour freshly boiled water over lime skin and sugar.
- Stir till sugar dissolves. Cover for 10 - 15 minutes. Cool.
- Cut limes crosswise and squeeze juice.
- Strain lime juice and syrup into a glass jug.
- Add cold water and mix well.
- Cool in refrigerator before serving.

Pineapple Drink

½ pineapple
840 ml/1½ pt cold water
90 g/3 oz/3 tbsp sugar
140 ml/¼ pt boiled water

- Put sugar into a bowl. Pour freshly boiled water over it. Stir till sugar dissolves. Cool.
- Grate pineapple and squeeze juice into a bowl.
- Strain juice and syrup into a glass jug.
- Add cold water and mix well. Taste.
- Cool in refrigerator before serving.

Variations

* You may use ½ sour sop or one cucumber and one lime in place of pineapple.

N.B. Left over pineapple pulp can be used to make pineapple jam. Refer to recipe of Pineapple Jam Tarts in Pastry section.

DRINKS

Syrup Milk Drink (Air Bandung)

280 ml/½ pt evaporated milk
280 ml/½ pt cold boiled water
90 g/3 oz/3 tbsp sugar
140 ml/¼ pt water ⎫ to make
½ tsp rose essence ⎬ syrup
a few drops red colouring ⎭

- Boil sugar and water till sugar dissolves.
- Add essence and colouring. Mix well. Strain and cool.
- Mix together syrup, milk and water in a glass jug.
- Cool in refrigerator before serving.

Variation

* You may use 560 ml/1 pt fresh milk without adding boiled water in place of evaporated milk.

Soyabean Milk

90 g/3 oz/3 tbsp soya beans soaked for 4 hours
1 litre/1¾ pt water
60 g/2 oz/2 tbsp sugar or to taste
2 screwpine leaves/pandan leaves – knotted

- Wash and remove skin from soya beans. Pound finely.
- Put soya beans to boil in water. Do not cover pot. Use low fire to simmer for 20 minutes.
- Strain. Boil with sugar and screwpine leaves till sugar dissolves.
- Remove screwpine leaves.
- Serve hot or cold.

Agar Drink (Minuman Agar-agar)

For Agar
30 g/1 oz agar (agar-agar)
560 ml/1 pt water
180 g/6 oz sugar
different colours to choice

For Syrup
90 g/3 oz/3 tbsp sugar
140 ml/¼ pt water
2 screwpine leaves/pandan leaves – knotted

Other Ingredients
560 ml/1 pt cold water
ice cubes

To Make Syrup
- Boil sugar, water and screwpine leaves till sugar dissolves. Cool.

To Make Agar
- Wash and soak agar for 10 minutes.
- Strain and boil with water till agar dissolves.
- When agar has dissolved, add sugar and simmer till sugar dissolves. Do not cover pot. Use low fire.
- Strain agar with muslin cloth.
- Divide agar into several portions. Add a different colour to each portion. Cool to set.
- When set, shred or grate agar. Mix together all the agar.

To Make Agar Drink
- Put agar in a glass till ½ full.
- Add syrup and cold water.
- Mix well and serve with ice cubes.

DRINKS

Egg Tea

1 egg per person
3 tsp fine sugar or to taste
280 ml/½ pt freshly boiled water

- Break egg into a cup.
- Add sugar and mix well.
- Pour in freshly boiled water and beat with a fork till sugar dissolves.
- Serve hot.

Egg Flip

1 egg
140 ml/¼ pt milk
1 tsp fine sugar or to taste
⅛ tsp vanilla essence

- Break egg in a bowl.
- Add sugar and beat with a fork till sugar dissolves.
- Heat milk but do not boil. Add egg.
- Add essence and mix well. Serve immediately.

Variation
* You may also add ½ tsp orange juice and ½ tsp orange peel into the egg flip.

Cream Style Corn Drink

½ tin cream style corn
560 ml/1 pt cold water
½ grated coconut to get 140 ml/¼ pt thick coconut milk
90 g/3 oz/3 tbsp sugar
140 ml/¼ pt water
1 screwpine leaf/*pandan* leaf – knotted

- Boil sugar with water and knotted screwpine leaf till sugar dissolves. Strain and cool.
- Pour cream style corn, syrup and thick coconut milk into a jug.
- Add enough cold water. Mix well. Taste.
- Cool in refrigerator before serving.

Barley Water

1 tbsp barley
840 ml/1½ pt water
2 tbsp sugar or to taste

- Wash barley and put in a pot with water.
- Bring to boil. Lower fire and simmer for one hour or till barley becomes soft.
- Add sugar and simmer till sugar dissolves.
- Strain in a jug and serve hot or cold.

Variation
* You may add lime juice before serving.

DESSERTS

DESSERTS

Stewed Pineapple

1 small pineapple
2 tbsp sugar or to taste
280 ml/½ pt water

- Cut pineapple into 1½ cm/½" cubes.
- Boil sugar with water.
- When sugar has dissolved, add pineapple.
- Lower fire and simmer for 10-15 minutes till pineapple becomes soft. Cool.
- Spoon into a fruit bowl or sundae glass. Cool in refrigerator.

Suggestion for Serving

* Stewed pineapple can be served with ice-cream or custard sauce. Refer to section on Sauces.

Variation

* Stewed pineapple can be used to make pineapple agar using method in Mixed Fruit Agar in this section which uses mixed fruits.

Water-melon Salad

½ small red water-melon
1 piece yellow water-melon
1 lime
2 dsp sugar or to taste
4 tbsp water
2 screwpine leaves/*pandan* leaves – knotted

- Boil sugar with water. When sugar has dissolved, add screwpine leaves and boil for a while. Cool.
- With a small round scoop, scoop out small red and yellow water-melon balls. Cut red water-melon shell like a bowl with serrated edge and stand shell on a plate.
- Put water-melon balls in the shell. Squeeze lime juice and pour syrup over water-melon balls. Mix well.
- Cool and serve with custard sauce separately. Refer to section on Sauces.

Variations

* Besides shaping into balls, water-melon can be cut into 2 cm/¾" cubes.
* Papaya can be used instead of water-melon.

DESSERTS

Mixed Fruits Salad

1 piece pineapple
1 piece papaya
2 bananas
juice from 1 lime
1½ tbsp sugar
6 tbsp water

- Cut pineapple into 1½ cm/½" cubes.
- Boil sugar with water.
- When sugar has dissolved, add pineapple. Simmer for five minutes. Cool.
- Cut papaya into 1½ cm/½" cubes.
- Cut bananas at a slant of suitable thickness. Add lime juice and mix well.
- Arrange fruits attractively in a fruit bowl and pour syrup over it or mix well and serve salad in sundae glasses.

Suggestions for Serving

* Mixed fruits salad can be served with custard sauce, ice-cream, evaporated milk or whipped cream.
* You may also add the following fruits:
  a piece of water melon – diced; one star fruit/carambola (*belimbing*) – cut as desired; one sapodilla (*ciku*) – cut as desired.

Red Beans Sweet (Bubur Kacang Merah)

90 g/3 oz red beans
180 g/6 oz/6 tbsp sugar or to taste
700 ml/1¼ pt water
2 screwpine leaves/*pandan* leaves – knotted
a pinch of salt

- Soak red beans for one hour. Strain.
- Boil red beans in water. When red beans become soft, add sugar.
- When sugar has dissolved, taste. Serve hot or cold.

Variations

* 1 tbsp soaked pearl sago (*sagu rumbia*) can be added before adding sugar.
* Dried orange peel can be used in place of screwpine leaves.

Suggestion for Serving

* You may serve red bean sweet with thick coconut milk separately.

DESSERTS

Green Beans Sweet
(Bubur Kacang Hijau)

90 g/3 oz green beans
½ grated coconut to get 140 ml/¼ pt
of thick coconut milk and 560 ml/1 pt
of thin coconut milk
60 g/2 oz/2 tbsp sugar or to taste
60 g/2 oz/2 tbsp chopped palm sugar
(*gula melaka*)
a pinch of salt
2 screwpine leaves/*pandan* leaves – knotted

- Soak green beans for one hour. Strain and boil with thin coconut milk and salt.
- When green beans become soft, add sugar and screwpine leaves.
- When sugar has dissolved, add thick coconut milk.
- When mixture boils, taste and turn off fire.
- Serve hot or cold.

Black Glutinous Rice Sweet
(Bubur Pulut Hitam)

2 tbsp black glutinous rice (*pulut hitam*)
½ grated coconut to get 140 ml/¼ pt
thick coconut milk and 560 ml/1 pt thin
coconut milk
4 full tbsp sugar or to taste
2 screwpine leaves/*pandan* leaves – knotted
a pinch of salt

- Boil black glutinous rice with thin coconut milk.
- When coconut milk boils, lower fire and simmer for ½ an hour till rice is soft. Stir now and then.
- Add sugar and screwpine leaves. Taste. When sugar has dissolved, remove screwpine leaves. Serve hot or cold.
- Mix thick coconut milk with a pinch of salt. Serve separately in a sauce boat or a bowl.

DESSERTS

Sweet Potato and Yam in Coconut Milk Sweet (Bubur Caca)

150 g/5 oz sweet potatoes
150 g/5 oz yam/taro (*keladi*)
5 - 6 tbsp sugar or to taste
½ grated coconut to get 560 ml/1 pt
of coconut milk
2 screwpine leaves/*pandan* leaves – knotted
a pinch of salt

- Cut away skin from sweet potatoes and yam. Dice.
- Steam yam and sweet potatoes for 10 minutes till soft.
- Boil coconut milk, sugar, salt and screwpine leaves.
- When coconut milk boils, add sweet potatoes and yam. Mix well. Taste.
- Serve hot or cold with ice.

Variations

* 1 dsp pearl sago (*sagu rumbia*) can be added.
* 60 g/2 oz/2 tbsp chopped palm sugar (*gula melaka*) may be added. In this case, reduce the other sugar by 2 tbsp.

Sweet Potato Soup

90 g/3 oz sweet potatoes with yellow flesh
90 g/3 oz sweet potatoes with red flesh
90 g/3 oz sweet potatoes with purple flesh
120 g/4 oz/4 tbsp sugar or to taste
700 ml/1¼ pt water
2 slices ginger
2 screwpine leaves/*pandan* leaves – knotted

- Cut away skin from sweet potatoes.
- Cut potatoes into cubes or wedges. Soak potatoes.
- Boil sweet potatoes, ginger, screwpine leaves and water.
- Lower fire and simmer for 5 - 10 minutes till sweet potatoes are soft.
- Add sugar and stir till sugar is dissolved. Taste. Serve hot or cold.

Variation

* Use 60 g/2 oz/2 tbsp brown sugar and 60 g/2 oz/2 tbsp sugar.

DESSERTS

Banana Snow (Pisang Salji)

3 bananas – *pisang emas* or any
suitable type
1 egg – use egg white only
juice of 1 lime
1 tbsp fine sugar or to taste
2 cherries for decoration

- Mash bananas. Mix this with sugar and lime juice.
- Whisk egg white till light and stiff.
- Fold in banana mixture little by little.
- Whisk mixture again till light and fluffy.
- Spoon mixture into sundae glasses.
- Decorate with a cherry. Cool in refrigerator before serving.

Variation
* Papaya can also be prepared in this way in place of banana.

Banana Sweet (Pengat Pisang)

4 bananas – *pisang raja* or any suitable type
½ grated coconut to get 140 ml/¼ pt
thick coconut milk and 420 ml/¾ pt
thin coconut milk
60 g/2 oz/2 tbsp chopped palm sugar
(*gula melaka*)
90 g/3 oz/3 tbsp sugar or to taste
2 screwpine leaves/*pandan* leaves – knotted
a pinch of salt

- Cut bananas to shape desired.
- Boil thin coconut milk with sugar, palm sugar and salt.
- When it boils, add bananas and screwpine leaves. Lower fire and simmer till soft. Stir now and then.
- Add thick coconut milk.
- When it boils again, turn off fire. Taste. Remove screwpine leaves.
- Serve hot or cold.

Semolina Sweet (Kesari)

120 g/4 oz/4 tbsp semolina (*suji*)
⅛ tsp salt
2 tbsp sugar
210 ml/⅜ pt milk
1 tbsp raisins
1 tbsp margarine/ghee (*minyak sapi*)
a few drops yellow colouring

- Using low fire, fry semolina without oil till golden brown. Stir all the time. Cool.
- Heat 1 tbsp margarine/ghee and sauté raisins using low fire. Dish out.
- Add sugar, milk and salt.
- When sugar has dissolved, sprinkle semolina on top and mix well till cooked and thickened. Turn off fire.
- Add raisins and yellow colouring. Mix well and pour in a greased tray.
- Press with a wooden spoon to flatten surface.
- Cool before cutting.

DESSERTS

Pearl Sago Pudding with Palm Sugar Syrup
(Puding Sagu Gula Melaka)

180 g/6 oz pearl sago (*sagu rumbia*)

For Sauce

½ grated coconut to get 140 ml/¼ pt
thick coconut milk
pinch of salt

For Syrup

60 g/2 oz/2 tbsp chopped palm sugar
(*gula melaka*)
60 g/2 oz/2 tbsp sugar
2 screwpine leaves/*pandan* leaves – knotted
70 ml/⅛ pt water

To Cook Pearl Sago

- Wash and soak pearl sago for 15 minutes. Strain.
- Boil water in a pot.
- When water boils, add pearl sago. Stir till pearl sago turns clear and transparent.
- Pour pearl sago into a sieve and wash under the tap to remove the extra starch.
- Allow pearl sago to set in rinsed moulds and keep in refrigerator.

To Cook Syrup

- Boil sugar and palm sugar in water till sugar dissolves.
- Add screwpine leaves and simmer for three minutes.
- Strain syrup into a sauce boat or suitable container.
- Mix thick coconut milk with salt and strain into a sauce boat or suitable container.
- Remove sago pudding from moulds.
- Serve with syrup and coconut milk separately.

DESSERTS

Cornflour Pudding with Coconut Milk (Puding Tepung Jagung dengan Santan)

30 g/1 oz cornflour (*tepung jagung*)
280 ml/½ pt coconut milk
45 g/1½ oz/1½ tbsp sugar
½ tsp vanilla essence
colouring to choice

- Blend cornflour with a little coconut milk.
- Heat remaining coconut milk in a rinsed saucepan.
- When coconut milk begins to boil, pour it over blended cornflour, stirring all the time.
- Rinse saucepan and pour mixture back into the saucepan.
- Using low fire and stirring all the time, cook until mixture thickens.
- Add sugar, essence and colouring. Mix well.
- Pour into rinsed moulds and cool.
- Serve with stewed pineapple. Refer to recipe of Stewed Pineapple in this section.

Variations

* These ingredients can be added to the pudding.
  (a) 2 *pisang emas*
     Remove skin and slice into 3 mm/⅛" pieces. Arrange in the mould and pour cooked cornflour mixture on it. Leave to set.
  (b) 1 *pisang raja* or any suitable cooking banana. Steam banana for 10 minutes.

Remove skin and cut slanting into 3 mm/⅛" pieces. Pour ½ quantity cooked cornflour mixture in the mould. Arrange pieces of banana on it and cover with the remaining cornflour mixture.
(c) Use milk in place of coconut milk.

Cream Style Corn Custard (Kastard Jagung)

30 g/1 oz/1 tbsp cornflour
⅛ grated coconut to get 210 ml/⅜ pt coconut milk
45 g/1½ oz/1½ tbsp sugar
1 tbsp cream style corn
½ tsp vanilla essence
colouring to choice

- Blend cornflour with a little coconut milk.
- Heat remaining coconut milk in a rinsed saucepan.
- When coconut milk begins to boil, pour it over blended cornflour, stirring all the time.
- Rinse saucepan. Pour mixture back into the saucepan.
- Using low fire and stirring all the time, cook mixture until it thickens.
- Add sugar, vanilla essence, colouring and cream style corn. Mix evenly.
- Pour this into a rinsed mould. Allow to cool and set. Serve with ice-cream or chocolate sauce. Refer to section on Sauces.

DESSERTS

Agar (Agar-agar) – Basic Recipe

7.5 g/¼ oz agar (*agar-agar*)
90 g/3 oz/3 tbsp sugar or to taste
420 ml/¾ pt water
2 screwpine leaves/*pandan* leaves – knotted
½ tsp vanilla essence
colouring to choice

- Wash and soak agar for 10 minutes. Strain.
- Boil agar in water using low fire till all the agar has dissolved.
- Do not cover pot after agar begins to boil.
- Add sugar and screwpine leaves and boil till sugar has dissolved.
- Strain agar with muslin cloth. Add vanilla essence and colouring. Mix well.
- Pour into rinsed moulds. Cool.
- Serve when agar has set.

Variations

* Lime Agar
  (a) Add lime juice to taste. Use green colouring and lemon essence.
* Mixed Fruits Agar
  (a) The following fruits can be added: 2 bananas; 1 piece pineapple; 1 piece papaya. Dice the fruits and put into the rinsed mould. Strain agar into the mould with fruits and leave to set.

* Pineapple Agar
  (a) Follow method in Mixed Fruits Agar but use stewed pineapple in place of mixed fruits. Refer to recipe of Stewed Pineapple in this section.

Chocolate Foam

7.5 g/¼ oz agar (*agar-agar*)
140 ml/¼ pt water
140 ml/¼ pt milk
90 g/3 oz/3 tbsp sugar or to taste
2 tsp cocoa
¼ tsp vanilla essence

- Wash and soak agar for 10 minutes. Strain.
- Boil agar in water using slow fire till agar dissolves. Do not cover saucepan after agar begins to boil.
- Strain agar with muslin cloth into a mixing bowl.
- Blend cocoa with a little milk. Heat remaining milk.
- When milk begins to boil, pour in blended cocoa.
- Boil cocoa mixture, sugar and vanilla essence till sugar has dissolved.
- When agar is nearly set, add cocoa mixture and beat till frothy. Pour agar into rinsed mould. Cool to set. Serve.

Variation

* Whisk egg white till light and stiff. Fold whisked egg white into beaten cocoa mixture.

DESSERTS

Magic Mirror (Agar-agar Cermin)

15 g/½ oz agar (*agar-agar*)
180 g/6 oz/6 tbsp sugar or to taste
700 ml/1¼ pt water
½ grated coconut to get 140 ml/¼ pt
of thick coconut milk
a pinch of salt
2 screwpine leaves/*pandan* leaves – knotted
suggested colouring – red, green and
yellow or to choice

- Wash and soak agar for 10 minutes. Strain.
- Add salt to coconut milk.
- Boil agar and water using low fire till all the agar has dissolved.
- Do not cover saucepan after agar begins to boil.
- Add sugar and screwpine leaves. Using low fire, boil till sugar dissolves.
- Strain with a muslin cloth and divide into two portions.
- Keep one portion warm by putting the bowl of agar in a plate containing hot water.
- Mix the second portion with coconut milk and divide again into three portions.
- Pour each portion into suitable-sized rinsed plates.
- Mix each portion evenly with a different colour, for instance red, green or yellow. Allow to set.
- When coloured agar has set, cut into 3 mm/⅛" cubes.
- Mix all the coloured agar cubes in a rinsed mould.
- Pour the uncoloured portion of agar into the mould.
- Leave to set. Serve.

DESSERTS

Coconut Milk Agar

7.5 g/¼ oz agar (*agar-agar*)
90 g/3 oz/3 tbsp sugar
½ grated coconut to get 140 ml/¼ pt
of coconut milk
280 ml/½ pt water
2 screwpine leaves/*pandan* leaves – knotted
a pinch of salt
colouring to choice

- Wash and soak agar for 10 minutes. Strain. Add a pinch of salt to coconut milk.
- Boil agar in water using low fire till all the agar dissolves. Do not cover saucepan after agar begins to boil.
- Add sugar and screwpine leaves.
- Boil again till sugar dissolves.
- Strain agar with muslin cloth and return to saucepan.
- Add coconut milk and colouring. When it boils, turn off fire.
- Pour into a rinsed mould. Cool.
- Serve when set.

Variation
* Use 60 g/2 oz/2 tbsp palm sugar (*gula melaka*) and 60 g/2 oz/2 tbsp sugar.

LOCAL KUIH

FRIED MASHED BANANA **122**
(JEMPUT PISANG)

STEAMED BANANA CAKE **122**
(LEPAT PISANG)

STEAMED TAPIOCA CAKE **124**
(LEPAT UBI KAYU)

SAVOURY FRIED TAPIOCA FRITTERS **124**
(CUCUR UBI KAYU)

SWEET POTATO DOUGHNUTS **125**
(KUIH KERIA)

PEARL SAGO CONES **126**
(ABUK-ABUK)

SAVOURY SWEET POTATO CAKE **128**
(KUIH BADAK)

SWEET GLUTINOUS RICE FLOUR BALLS **129**
(BUAH MELAKA)

FRIED LENTIL CAKE **129**
(VADAI)

SWEET POTATO SNOW BALLS **130**
(ONDE-ONDE)

FRIED GREEN BEAN BALLS **132**
(KUIH RENGAS/KUIH KASTURI)

SPECKLED GLUTINOUS RICE FLOUR BALLS **133**
(KUIH BIJAN)

STEAMED GLUTINOUS RICE WITH GRATED COCONUT TOPPING **134**
(PULUT INTI)

GRILLED GLUTINOUS RICE WITH DRIED SHRIMPS **136**
(PULUT UDANG PANGGANG)

STEAMED GLUTINOUS RICE WITH COCONUT MILK CUSTARD TOPPING **138**
(SERI MUKA)

STEAMED YAM CAKE **140**

STEAMED SMALL CUP SPONGE **141**
(APAM)

BAKED SMALL CUP SPONGE **142**
(KUIH BAULU)

STEAMED SPONGE **144**

LOCAL KUIH

Fried Mashed Banana
(Jemput Pisang)

3 *pisang raja* or any type of banana suitable
for cooking
3 dsp sugar or to taste
4 - 6 dsp wheat flour (*tepung gandum*)
⅛ tsp salt
1 tbsp grated white coconut – optional
1 large bowl oil

- Mash bananas lightly.
- Mix together with other ingredients and sift in enough flour to get a dropping consistency.
- Drop mixture spoonful by spoonful into heated oil.
- Deep fry till golden brown. Drain and serve.

Variation
* You may use ripe papaya in place of banana.

Steamed Banana Cake
(Lepat Pisang)

4 *pisang raja* or any type of banana suitable
for cooking
2 tbsp grated white coconut – optional
1 - 2 tbsp wheat flour (*tepung gandum*)
2 tbsp sugar or to taste
⅛ tsp salt
2 screwpine leaves/*pandan* leaves – cut into
5 cm/2" lengths
8 - 10 banana leaves 15 × 20 cm/6 × 8" in
size – softened in boiling water

- Mash bananas lightly.
- Mix together with all the other ingredients and enough sifted flour to get a thick mixture.
- Divide mixture into 8 - 10 portions.
- Spoon one portion onto a banana leaf.
- Place a piece of screwpine leaf on top of mixture.
- Fold banana leaf to enclose mixture. Follow photographs and instructions.
- Steam for 10 - 15 minutes till cooked.
- Leave to cool and serve.

To Wrap Banana Mixture
* Refer to photographs and instructions given.

LOCAL KUIH

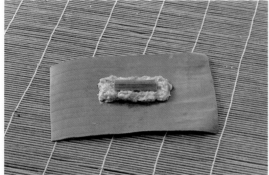

(i)   Place banana leaf with shiny side on flat surface. Spoon one portion of mixture on banana leaf. Shape into a rectangle. Place a pandan leaf on top of mixture.

(ii)   Fold the banana leaf to cover mixture.

(iii) Fold the other side of the banana leaf on top.

(iv)   Fold the two sides over. Place folded sides under.

LOCAL KUIH

Steamed Tapioca Cake (Lepat Ubi Kayu)

150 g/5 oz tapioca/cassava (*ubi kayu*)
¼ grated white coconut
3 tbsp sugar or to taste
¼ tsp salt
1 - 2 tsp thick coconut milk
¼ tsp *pandan* essence
a few drops green or yellow colouring
2 screwpine leaves/*pandan* leaves cut into 5 cm/2" in length
8 - 10 banana leaves 15 × 20 cm/6 × 8" in size – softened in boiling water

- Remove skin and grate tapioca. Squeeze grated tapioca to remove juice.
- Mix grated tapioca with all the other ingredients to form a soft mixture.
- Divide into 8 - 10 portions. Spoon one portion on banana leaf. Place a piece of *pandan* leaf on top of the mixture.
- Fold the banana leaf to enclose mixture. Follow photographs and instructions for Steamed Banana Cake (*Lepat Pisang*) in this section.
- Steam for 10 - 15 minutes till cooked.
- Leave to cool. Serve.

Savoury Fried Tapioca Fritters (Cucur Ubi Kayu)

60 g/2 oz/2 tbsp wheat flour (*tepung gandum*)
⅛ tsp salt or to taste
1 tsp curry powder – optional
1 egg
70 ml/⅛ pt water or coconut milk
150 g/5 oz tapioca/cassava (*ubi kayu*)
1 tbsp dried shrimps (*udang kering*)
1 red chilli
1 stalk spring onion
4 shallots
1 large bowl of oil for deep frying

- Soak, strain and chop finely dried shrimps.
- Slice shallots finely lengthwise. Slice chilli finely. Chop spring onion.
- Grate tapioca and squeeze to remove juice.
- Sift flour. Add salt and curry powder (if used).
- Make a well in the centre. Drop in egg and add water or coconut milk. Beat until mixture is smooth.
- Add vegetables, tapioca and dried shrimps. Mix thoroughly.
- Drop spoonfuls of mixture into heated oil and deep fry till golden brown.
- Drain and serve with sauce. Refer to section on Sauces.

Variation

* You may use 90 g/3 oz of prawns in place of dried shrimps.

LOCAL KUIH

Sweet Potato Doughnuts
(Kuih Keria)

For Sweet Potato Dough
300 g/10 oz sweet potatoes
with yellow flesh
3 dsp or more wheat flour (*tepung gandum*)

For Sugar Coating
2 tbsp sugar
1 tbsp water

Other Ingredient
1 large bowl oil for deep frying

To Make Dough

- Scrub and wash sweet potatoes.
- Boil sweet potatoes in their jackets for 20 - 30 minutes till cooked.
- Remove potato skin. Mash potatoes till fine.
- Sift enough flour onto mashed potatoes. Mix into a pliable dough that does not stick to fingers. If dough is too dry, add a little water.

To Make Doughnut

- Shape dough into a sausage roll of about 4 cm/1½" in diameter.
- Divide dough into 8 - 10 equal pieces.
- Shape each piece into a smooth, flat round piece of about 2 cm/¾" thick.
- Make a hole in the centre of the flat round piece like a doughnut. Smoothen the surface.
- Repeat till all the pieces are done.
- Heat oil.
- Deep fry the sweet potato doughnuts till golden brown. Drain well.

- Drain oil from frying pan/wok.
- Put in sugar and water. Allow to boil till sugar dissolves to get a very thick syrup. Lower fire.
- Put in the doughnuts and toss lightly so that they are well-coated with the thick syrup. Continue to stir until syrup crystalises.
- Cool doughnuts before serving.

LOCAL KUIH

Pearl Sago Cones (Abuk-abuk)

120 g/4 oz/4 tbsp pearl sago
(*sagu rumbia*)
4 tbsp grated white coconut
⅛ tsp salt
4 screwpine leaves/*pandan* leaves to get
1 tbsp thick *pandan* juice or ¼ tsp
pandan essence
a few drops green colouring
1½ tbsp finely chopped palm ⎫
sugar (*gula melaka*) ⎬ mix together
1½ tbsp sugar ⎭
4 - 5 banana leaves 20 cm/8" square –
softened in boiling water

- Wash and soak pearl sago for about 15 minutes.
- Strain pearl sago and mix thoroughly with grated coconut, salt, *pandan* juice or *pandan* essence and colouring.
- Divide sago mixture into 16 - 20 portions and sugar mixture into 8 - 10 portions.

- Prepare banana cones. Refer to steps shown in the photographs below.
- Spoon one portion of sago mixture into cone and press lightly to fill up tip of cone.
- Make a hole in the sago mixture and put in one portion of sugar mixture.
- Cover with another portion of sago mixture. Press lightly.
- Fold the cone to get a firm base. Refer to photographs shown.
- Steam for 15 - 20 minutes till pearl sago becomes transparent and cooked.

Variations

* This mixtures can be cooked in a tray. Divide mixture into two portions. Mix each portion with a different colour. Put one portion in tray and spread it out evenly. Sprinkle sugar mixture evenly on top. Spoon second portion over sugar evenly. Steam it till cooked and sago becomes clear. Cool before cutting.

(i) Cut the square banana leaf into two triangles. Form a cone with one triangular leaf. Cut top edge evenly.

(ii) Spoon pearl sago mixture into cone.

(iii) Fold cone to get a firm base.

LOCAL KUIH

Savoury Sweet Potato Cake (Kuih Badak)

For Sweet Potato Dough
300 g/10 oz sweet potatoes
with yellow flesh
3 dsp or more of wheat flour (*tepung gandum*)

For Filling
2 dried chillies
1 tsp fennel (*jintan manis*)
1½ cm/½" cube dry turmeric (*kunyit kering*)
1 tbsp dried shrimps (*udang kering*)
¼ grated white coconut
4 shallots
2 slices ginger
1 red chilli
1 stick lemon grass (*serai*)
½ tsp salt or to taste
2 tbsp oil

Other Ingredient
1 large bowl of oil for deep frying

To Make Filling
- Wash and strain dried shrimps.
- Finely slice lemon grass. Slice shallots finely lengthwise.
- Finely dice ginger and red chilli.
- Wipe dried chillies with a dry cloth.
- Heat pan/wok. Fry dried chillies, dry turmeric and fennel without oil, using low fire.
- Immediately use a dry pounder to pound the mixture into fine powder. Spoon out.
- Pound dried shrimps.
- Heat oil. Lower fire. Fry chilli powder mixture until there is nice aroma.

- Add dried shrimps and fry till you get nice aroma. Add grated coconut, shallots, ginger, red chilli, lemon grass and salt. Mix well. Taste.

To Make Dough
* Refer to recipe of Sweet Potato Doughnut (*Kuih Keria*) in this section.

To Make Savoury Sweet Potato Cake
- Shape dough into a sausage roll of about 4 cm/1½" in diameter.
- Divide dough into 8 - 10 equal pieces.
- Roll one piece of dough into a ball and shape to form a small bowl.
- Fill centre of bowl with enough filling. Cover up filling with the dough.
- Shape the dough neatly again to form a flat round piece of 2 cm/¾" thick.
- Deep fry in heated oil till golden brown.
- Drain and serve.

LOCAL KUIH

Sweet Glutinous Rice Flour Balls (Buah Melaka)

For Dough
90 g/3 oz/3 tbsp dry glutinous rice flour (*tepung pulut*)
¼ tsp salt
2 - 4 tbsp water
¼ tsp *pandan* essence
a few drops green colouring

For Filling
1 dsp finely chopped palm sugar (*gula melaka*)
1 dsp sugar
} mix together

For Coating
¼ grated coconut
¼ tsp salt
} mix together

- Sift together glutinous rice flour and salt.
- Add in sufficient water, *pandan* essence and colouring. Mix well to get a pliable dough which does not stick to fingers.
- Cover dough with a damp cloth and leave for at least 15 minutes.
- Shape dough into a sausage roll of 2 cm/ ¾" in diameter.
- Cut dough into 2 cm/¾" pieces. Roll each piece into a ball. Flatten each ball into a thin piece.
- Spoon a little sugar onto the centre.
- Cover up the sugar with the dough. Roll to reshape.
- Place balls in boiling water.
- Glutinous rice flour balls float when cooked.
- Dish balls out with a perforated ladle.
- Toss balls in grated coconut.
- For serving refer to recipe of Sweet Potato Snow Balls in this section.

Fried Lentil Cake (Vadai)

120 g/4 oz/4 tbsp lentils (*kacang dal*) – soaked for at least 4 hours
1 green chilli
1 sprig curry leaf
½ onion
1 tsp fennel (*jintan manis*)
½ tsp salt or to taste
1 large bowl oil for deep fat frying
1 banana leaf

- Strain lentils which have been soaked. Pound ¾ lentils finely and the remainder coarsely.
- Dice finely chilli and onion. Shred finely curry leaf.
- Mix together the lentils, chilli, curry leaf, onion, fennel and salt.
- Divide mixture into 8 - 10 portions.
- Put one portion on the greased banana leaf.
- Shape each portion into a flattened round, with the outer edge thinner than the centre.
- Deep fry in heated oil till golden brown. Drain and serve.

LOCAL KUIH

Sweet Potato Snow Balls
(Onde-onde)

For Dough

150 g/5 oz sweet potatoes with yellow flesh
2 dsp wheat flour (*tepung gandum*)
4 screwpine leaves/*pandan* leaves to get
1 tbsp thick *pandan* juice or ¼ tsp *pandan*
essence
a few drops of green colouring

For Filling

1 dsp finely chopped palm sugar ⎫
(*gula melaka*)   ⎬ mix together
1 dsp sugar   ⎭

For Coating

¼ grated white coconut ⎫
                        ⎬ mix together
¼ tsp salt   ⎭

To Make Dough

- Scrub and wash sweet potatoes. Do not peel the skin.
- Boil sweet potatoes for 15 - 20 minutes until cooked.
- Remove potato skin. Mash potatoes till fine.
- Sift enough flour onto mashed potatoes.
- Add in *pandan* juice or *pandan* essence and colouring.
- Mix into a pliable dough that does not stick to fingers. Add more flour if necessary.

To Make Sweet Potato Snow Balls

- Shape dough into a sausage roll of 2 cm/¾" in diameter.
- Cut dough into 2 cm/¾" pieces.
- Roll each piece into a ball. Flatten each ball into a thin round piece and spoon a little sugar mixture onto the centre.
- Cover up the sugar with the dough. Roll to reshape.
- Place balls in boiling water.
- Potato snow balls float when cooked.
- Dish balls out with a perforated ladle.
- Toss balls in grated coconut.
- Arrange sweet potato snow balls on plate.

Suggestions for Serving

* Arrange sweet potato snow balls in a banana leaf basket.
* Arrange sweet potato snow balls in a cone.

To Make Banana Leaf Basket

- Refer to photographs and instructions given.

(i)   *Cut banana leaf into a 11½ cm/4½" square. Snip 2 cm/¾" from edge on two opposite sides.*

(ii) *Fold up unsnipped side to enclose snipped corners and staple sides together.*

LOCAL KUIH

(iii) A finished banana leaf basket.

(i)   Cut softened banana leaf into 15 cm/6" square. Fold one side over to form a cone. Trim base of cone evenly.

To Prepare a Cone

* Refer to photographs and instructions given.

(ii)   A finished cone.

LOCAL KUIH

Fried Green Bean Balls
(Kuih Rengas/Kuih Kasturi)

For Green Bean Mixture
90 g/3 oz/3 tbsp green beans – soak for at
least 4 hours
420 ml/¾ pt water
¼ tsp salt
1½ tbsp palm sugar (*gula melaka*)
1½ tbsp sugar
2 screwpine leaves/*pandan* leaves – knotted

For Coating Green Bean Mixture
2 tbsp dry rice flour (*tepung beras*)
⅛ tsp salt
4 - 6 tbsp water
⅛ tsp slake lime (*kapur*)

Other Ingredient
1 large bowl oil for deep fat frying

To Cook Green Beans
- Strain beans.
- Boil beans till soft.
- Lower fire and simmer till almost dry.
- Stir to prevent beans from sticking to pan/wok.
- Add sugar, salt and screwpine leaves. Stir until mixture is thick but not dry.
- Remove screwpine leaves.
- Cool mixture.

To Make Green Bean Balls
- Make dough into balls of about 4 cm/1½" in diameter.
- Flatten balls desired.

To Prepare Coating Batter
- Sift rice flour and salt.
- Add enough water and mix evenly to get a thick batter.
- Add slake lime. Mix well.

To Cook Green Bean Balls
- Coat balls/rounds of green bean mixture with batter.
- Straight away deep fry balls in heated oil till golden brown.
- Use low fire to fry. Drain and serve.

LOCAL KUIH

Speckled Glutinous Rice Flour Balls (Kuih Bijan)

For Dough
120 g/4 oz/4 tbsp dry glutinous rice flour
(*tepung pulut*)
¼ tsp salt
4 - 6 tbsp water

For Coconut Filling
¼ grated white coconut
3 dsp chopped palm sugar (*gula melaka*)
3 dsp sugar
3 dsp water
¼ tsp salt
2 screwpine leaves/*pandan* leaves – knotted

Other Ingredients
4 tbsp sesame seeds – remove any grains of
sand or foreign matter
1 large bowl oil for deep fat frying

To Prepare Dough
- Sift together glutinous rice flour and salt.
- Add sufficient water to get a pliable dough which does not stick to fingers.
- Cover dough with a damp cloth and leave for at least 15 minutes.

To Prepare Coconut Filling
- Refer to recipe on Steamed Glutinous Rice With Grated Coconut Topping (*Pulut Inti*) in this section.

To Prepare Speckled Glutinous Rice Flour Balls
- Shape dough into a sausage roll of 4 cm/ 1½" in diameter.
- Cut dough into 1½ cm/½" pieces.

- Press out each piece of dough as thin as possible.
- Spoon a little coconut mixture onto the centre.
- Cover up the filling with the dough. Roll to reshape.
- Toss glutinous rice flour balls in sesame seeds.
- Press sesame seeds lightly onto surface of balls.
- Deep fry in heated oil till golden brown.
- Drain and serve.

N.B. For sesame seeds to stick more easily, dip the glutinous rice flour balls in water before tossing in sesame seeds.

LOCAL KUIH

Steamed Glutinous Rice with Grated Coconut Topping (*Pulut Inti*)

For Steamed Glutinous Rice

300 g/10 oz glutinous rice (*pulut*)
– soak for at least 4 hours
½ grated coconut to get 280 ml/½ pt
coconut milk
½ tsp salt
2 screwpine leaves/*pandan* leaves – knotted

For Grated Coconut Topping

¼ grated white coconut
3 dsp chopped palm sugar (*gula melaka*)
3 dsp sugar
3 dsp water
¼ tsp salt
2 screwpine leaves/*pandan* leaves – knotted
8 - 10 banana leaves 20 cm/8" square –
softened in boiling water

To Cook Glutinous Rice

- Mix ½ tsp salt to coconut milk.
- Strain glutinous rice. Add in enough coconut milk just to cover the rice.
- Place knotted screwpine leaves on top.
- Steam for 20 - 30 minutes till cooked.
- Remove screwpine leaves. Stir glutinous rice and divide into 8 - 10 portions.

To Make Grated Coconut Topping

- Boil sugar with water till sugar dissolves.
- Add grated coconut and knotted screwpine leaves. Stir mixture till grated coconut has absorbed syrup and mixture is moist.
- Remove screwpine leaves. Divide into 8 – 10 portions.

To Wrap Pulut Inti

* Refer to photographs and instructions given.

(i) Cut softened banana leaves into required measurement. Place one portion of glutinous rice on banana leaf. Shape neatly into a rectangle. Place one portion of grated coconut topping on top of glutinous rice.

(ii) Fold one corner of banana leaf over rice and topping.

(iii) Fold the opposite corner of the same end over.

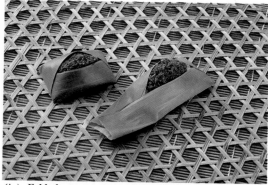

(iv) Fold the two corners of the other end in the reverse order. Fold the two ends to form a piramid.

LOCAL KUIH

Grilled Glutinous Rice with Dried Shrimps (Pulut Udang Panggang)

For Steamed Glutinous Rice

300 g/10 oz glutinous rice (*pulut*)
– soaked for at least 4 hours
½ grated coconut to get 280 ml/½ pt
of coconut milk
½ tsp salt
2 screwpine leaves/*pandan* leaves – knotted

For Filling

2 dried chillies
1 tsp fennel (*jintan manis*)
1/½ cm/½" cube dry turmeric
(*kunyit kering*)
1 tbsp dried shrimps (*udang kering*)
¼ grated white coconut
4 shallots
2 slices ginger
1 red chilli
1 stick lemon grass (*serai*)
½ tsp salt or to taste
2 tbsp oil
8 - 10 banana leaves 15 × 20 cm/6 × 8" in
size – softened in boiling water

To Cook Glutinous Rice

• Refer to recipe of Steamed Glutinous Rice with Grated Coconut Topping (*Pulut Inti*) in this section.

To Make Filling

• Refer to recipe of Savoury Sweet Potato Cake (*Kuih Badak*) in this section.

To Make Grilled Glutinous Rice with Dried Shrimps

• Divide glutinous rice into 8 - 10 portions.
• Wrap rice and filling by following photographs and instructions given.

• Grill glutinous rice on both sides before serving.

To Wrap Glutinous Rice

• Refer to photographs and instructions given.

(i)   Cut softened banana leaf to required measurement. Spoon one portion of glutinous rice onto a banana leaf. Shape it into a rectangle.

(ii) Spoon enough filling onto half section of rectangle but keep slightly away from edges.

(iii) Bring over the other half of glutinous rice to cover the filling.

(iv) *Cover glutinous rice with one side of banana leaf. Press lightly and shape into a sausage with the banana leaf. Wrap glutinous rice with the banana leaf.*

(v) *Fold in the two shorter sides of banana leaf and seal the edges with stapler.*

LOCAL KUIH

Steamed Glutinous Rice with Coconut Milk Custard Topping (Seri Muka)

For Glutinous Rice Layer

300 g/10 oz glutinous rice (*pulut*) – soaked for at least 4 hours
½ grated coconut to get 280 ml/½ pt coconut milk
½ tsp salt
2 screwpine leaves/*pandan* leaves – knotted

For Custard (*seri kaya*) – Top Layer

3 eggs
180 g/6 oz sugar or to taste
1 grated coconut to get 210 ml/⅜ pt of thick coconut milk
⅛ tsp salt
¼ tsp *pandan* essence
a few drops of yellow or green colouring

Utensil

a steaming tray 15 cm/6" in diameter and 5 cm/2" in height

Other Ingredient

1 banana leaf

To Prepare Glutinous Rice – For Bottom Layer

- Refer to recipe of Steamed Glutinous Rice With Grated Coconut Topping (*Pulut Inti*) in this section.

To Prepare Custard – For Top Layer

- Beat egg with sugar till sugar is dissolved.
- Add in thick coconut milk, essence and colouring. Mix well and strain.

To Cook Top Layer

- When bottom layer of glutinous rice is cooked, remove tray from steamer.
- Press the glutinous rice with a banana leaf to get a firm layer and even surface.
- Return tray to steamer and steam glutinous rice for a few minutes.
- Stir egg mixture and pour straight on top of glutinous rice.
- Steam again for 20 - 30 minutes till top layer is cooked. Use low fire.
- Avoid condensed water from steamer falling on surface of custard by covering tray with a grease proof paper or wiping steamer lid occasionally.
- When the top layer is cooked, it looks like egg custard.
- Cool the cake thoroughly before cutting into suitable sizes. Dish out to serve.

Suggestion

* Use blue colouring to colour a portion of glutinous rice after rice is soaked and strained. Then mix with remaining glutinous rice to form a blue pattern or strips on glutinous rice when cooked.

N.B. The top layer can be used as a spread for sandwiches and pancakes.

LOCAL KUIH

Steamed Yam Cake

Batter Mixture

180 g/6 oz/6 tbsp dry rice flour
(*tepung beras*)
¼ tsp salt
560 ml/1 pt water
½ tsp alkali water
300 g/10 oz yam/taro (*keladi*)
½ tsp five-spice powder – optional
2 tbsp dried shrimps (*udang kering*)
8 tbsp oil
slake lime (*kapur*)

For Garnishing

1 stalk spring onion
2 red chillies finely chopped
8 shallots – fried

Utensil

pyrex dish or a steaming tray 15 cm/6" in
diameter and 5 cm/2" high

- Sift together rice flour and salt into a mixing bowl.
- Make a well in the centre. Pour in 280 ml/ ½ pt water. Mix well. If too thick add more liquid. Beat mixture till smooth.
- Add another 280 ml/½ pt water and mix well. Allow to stand for 20 - 30 minutes.
- Soak, strain and chop finely dried shrimps. Dice yam into 1½ cm/½" cubes. Slice shallots crosswise.
- Heat oil. Fry shallots till golden brown. Dish out.
- Sauté dried shrimps till you get nice aroma. Add yam cubes and five-spice powder (if used). Fry for two minutes.
- Heat tray in steamer.

- Mix batter with slake lime.
- Add fried yam mixture into batter. Mix well.
- Pour in the batter mixture onto the steaming tray when it is heated up.
- Steam for 20 - 30 minutes until cooked.
- Immediately garnish with finely chopped chillies, spring onion and fried shallots that have been mixed together.
- Thoroughly cool cooked yam cake before cutting into suitable pieces for serving.
- Serve with chilli sauce. Refer to section on Sauces.

LOCAL KUIH

Steamed Small Cup Sponge
(Apam)

1 egg
1 tsp vanilla essence
90 g/3 oz castor sugar
90 g/3 oz wheat flour (*tepung gandum*)
70 ml/⅛ pt ice-cream soda
colouring to choice

- Line patitin with cake cups.
- Sift flour.
- Whisk egg till fluffy.
- Add sugar and vanilla essence. Whisk till thick and fluffy.
- Sift in flour, half quantity at a time and fold in evenly with a metal spoon.
- Divide mixture into 3 portions.
- Add colouring and ⅓ ice-cream soda to one portion of mixture. Fold in evenly.
- Fold in remaining ice-cream soda into the remaining 2 portions.
- Fill plain mixture into cups till ⅔ full.
- Add coloured mixture on top till nearly full.
- Steam sponge for 15 minutes till cooked, risen and cracked on surface.
- Remove from steamer. Leave for two minutes before cooling on rack.

LOCAL KUIH

Baked Small Cup Sponge
(Kuih Baulu)

2 eggs
60 g/2 oz castor sugar
60 g/2 oz wheat flour (*tepung gandum*)
1 tsp rice flour
½ tsp baking powder
a pinch of salt
patitin or *kuih baulu* mould

- Line patitin with cake cups or grease *kuih baulu* mould.
- Sift wheat flour, rice flour, baking powder and salt.
- Whisk eggs with sugar till light and fluffy.
- Sift half quantity of flour over mixture and lightly fold flour into mixture with a metal spoon. Repeat with remaining flour.
- Fill cup ⅔ full.
- Bake in preheated oven 190ºC/375ºF/5 for 10 - 15 minutes till golden brown.
- Remove from oven. Leave for 2 - 3 minutes before cooling on rack.

LOCAL KUIH

Steamed Sponge

3 eggs
120 g/4 oz castor sugar
120 g/4 oz wheat flour (*tepung gandum*)
1 tsp baking powder
1 tsp vanilla essence

- Sift flour and baking powder.
- Whisk egg and sugar till thick and fluffy.
- Sift in half quantity of flour and fold in evenly.
- Repeat with remaining flour and vanilla essence.
- Pour mixture into a greased baking tin or pyrex dish.
- Cover tin or dish with grease-proof paper.
- Steamed for 20 - 30 minutes till cooked.
- Leave to stand in tin or dish for a short while.
- Remove sponge from tin or dish and cool on rack before serving.

BREAD

SCRAMBLE EGGS ON TOAST 146

CHEESE ON TOAST 146

BOMBAY TOAST 146

FRENCH TOAST 146

SANDWICHES – BASIC RECIPE 147

DOUBLE DECKER SANDWICH 148

PRAWNS ON TOAST 150

SARDINE ON TOAST 150

BREAD

Scramble Eggs on Toast

4 slices buttered toast
2 eggs
2 tbsp milk
1 tsp margarine/butter
salt & pepper to taste

- Beat eggs with milk, salt and pepper.
- Heat a small saucepan and add in margarine.
- When margarine has melted, pour in egg mixture. Lower fire.
- Keep stirring with a wooden spoon till eggs thicken but moist.
- Serve hot on buttered toast.

Bombay Toast

4 slices bread
2 small eggs/1 big egg
2 tbsp milk
pinch of salt & pepper
½ rice bowl oil

- Beat eggs with milk and salt.
- Heat oil in wok.
- Dip both sides of bread in egg mixture.
- Put bread in oil. Lower fire.
- Fry till both sides of bread are golden brown.
- Serve with marmite, vegemite or bovril.

Cheese on Toast

4 slices toast
1 tbsp butter/margarine
4 slices cheese
2 tomatoes

- Butter toast.
- Slice tomatoes.
- Arrange sliced tomatoes on top of toast. Cover with cheese.
- Grill cheese until it becomes soft.
- Serve hot.

French Toast

4 slices bread
2 small eggs/1 big egg
2 tbsp milk
1 tbsp sugar or according to taste
½ rice bowl oil

- Beat eggs and milk with sugar till sugar dissolves.
- Heat oil in wok.
- Dip both sides of bread in egg mixture.
- Put bread in oil. Lower fire.
- Fry till both sides of bread are golden brown.
- Leave out sugar if served with jam, honey, treacle or golden syrup.

BREAD

Sandwiches — Basic Recipe

½ loaf sandwich bread
filling according to choice
2 dsp butter/margarine
¼ cucumber

- Make filling and slice cucumber thinly.
- Beat butter to soften it.
- Divide filling according to number of sandwiches to be made.
- Spread butter and filling on one slice of bread. Arrange cucumber on filling. Cover with the other slice of buttered bread. Press lightly.
- Repeat the above process until all the bread is finished.
- Cut away sides of bread.
- Cut according to desired shape. Serve.

Suggested Sandwich Fillings

* Egg Filling

2 hard-boiled eggs
1 tbsp mayonnaise
1 tsp butter/margarine
salt & pepper to taste

Mash eggs with fork. Add in mayonnaise, butter, salt and pepper. Mix evenly to a paste.

* Egg Omelette Filling – Refer to recipe of Egg Omelette in section on Eggs.

* Sardine Filling – Refer to recipe of Sardine Roll Filling in Pastry section.

* Dried Shrimp *Sambal* Filling – Refer to recipe of Dried Shrimp *Sambal* in Fish section.

* Dry Curry Meat Filling – Refer to recipe of Curry Puff Filling in Pastry section.

* Anchovy *Sambal* Filling – Refer to recipe of Anchovy Sambal (*Sambal Ikan Bilis*) in Fish section.

* Meat *Rendang* Filling — Refer to recipe of Meat *Rendang*/Spicy Meat in Coconut Milk (*Rendang Daging*) in Meat Section.

* Grated Coconut Filling – Refer to recipe of Steamed Glutinous Rice with Grated Coconut Topping (*Pulut Inti*) in Local *Kuih* Section.

* *Seri Muka* Filling – Refer to recipe of Steamed Glutinous Rice with Coconut Milk Custard Topping (*Seri Muka*) in Local Kuih Section. Follow steps for preparing custard of top layer. Strain egg mixture and pour into container. Steam for about half an hour till set. You may use knotted fresh screwpine leaves/*pandan* leaves in place of *pandan* essence. Remove leaves before mixture is set.

BREAD

Double Decker Sandwich

8 pieces sandwich bread
½ quantity sardine filling
½ quantity egg filling
½ small carrot
salt to taste
2 tbsp butter/margarine
aluminium foil

- Make egg and sardine fillings. Refer to recipe of Egg Filling in this section and Sardine Roll Filling in Pastry section.
- To make carrot filling. Grate carrot. Add salt and 1 tsp butter. Mix evenly to a paste. Add more butter if necessary.
- Divide bread into two sets of four slices each.
- Make sardine and egg sandwiches. Before putting sardine sandwich on egg sandwich, spread butter before spreading carrot filling in between. Press lightly.
- Wrap in foil and freeze for at least two hours or overnight.
- Take out from freezer. Thaw. Cut away sides of bread.
- Cut into fingers or rectangular shape. Serve.

(i)   Make sardine and egg sandwiches.

(ii)   Spread butter and carrot filling on egg sandwich. Spread butter on sardine sandwich.

(iii)   Place sardine sandwich on egg sandwich.

(iv)   Trim the sides and cut into fingers.

BREAD

Prawns on Toast

½ loaf bread
240 g/8 oz prawns
1 small egg
1 tsp cornflour
1 onion
½ rice bowl bread crumbs
salt and pepper to taste
1 bowl oil for deep frying
chilli sauce

- Chop prawns and onion separately.
- Beat egg.
- Trim sides of bread and cut into four.
- Mix together prawns, egg, cornflour, onion, salt and pepper.
- Divide mixture according to pieces of bread.
- Spread mixture on each piece of bread.
- Cover prawn mixture with bread crumbs.
- Heat oil. Put in bread, surface with the mixture prawn to the oil. Lower fire.
- Fry till golden brown. Turn over and fry the other side till golden brown.
- Serve hot with chilli sauce.

N.B. You may serve with instant chilli sauce, chilli tomato sauce, chilli garlic sauce or chilli shrimp paste sauce (*sambal belacan*). Refer to section on Sauces.

Sardine on Toast

4 slices toast
1 small tin sardine
½ tsp lime juice
2 tsp butter/margarine
salt & pepper to taste

- Remove bones from sardine and mash with a fork.
- Add lime juice and enough sardine sauce. Mix evenly to a paste.
- Heat wok. Add margarine.
- Add sardine, salt and pepper. Mix well.
- Serve hot on buttered toast.

BATTER

BATTER

Thin Batter Using Wheat Flour
– Basic Recipe

120 g/4 oz/4 tbsp wheat flour (*tepung gandum*)
¼ tsp salt
1 egg
280 ml/½ pt liquid

- Sift wheat flour and salt into a mixing bowl.
- Make a well in the centre.
- Break in egg. Add in ½ quantity of liquid.
- Mix to a smooth consistency. Do not allow the mixture to be doughy or lumpy.
- If batter is too thick, add more liquid, a little at a time.
- When the mixture is smooth, beat the batter for a few minutes until bubbles appear on the surface.
- Add in remaining liquid and mix well.
- Allow the batter to stand for 20-30 minutes before use.

N.B. Milk, syrup or coconut milk can be used as liquid for the batter.

BATTER

Jam Pancake

For Batter
120 g/4 oz/4 tbsp wheat flour (*tepung gandum*)
¼ tsp salt
1 egg
280 ml/½ pt milk
yellow colouring if desired
2 - 3 tbsp jam
1 tbsp margarine/butter

To Make Batter
- Follow basic recipe of Thin Batter Using Wheat Flour.
- Add colouring together with second quantity of milk.

To Make Pancake
- Heat pan lightly. Use a crushed grease proof paper to grease the pan with a little margarine or butter.
- Stir batter well.

- Use a ladle to pour enough batter into pan. Rotate pan to get a thin round pancake.
- Do not over heat pan. Use low fire.
- When the under-side is golden brown, loosen the edges and turn over to cook the other side.
- When cooked, remove pancake to a flat plate.
- Immediately spread with jam.
- Roll or fold pancake. Serve.

Suggestion For Serving
* Instead of jam, serve pancake with honey, treacle, golden syrup, marmite, bovril, vegemite or coconut egg custard. Refer to recipe of Steamed Glutinous Rice with Coconut Milk Custard Topping (*Seri Muka*) in Local Kuih section.
* Pancake can also be served with lime juice and sugar. When pancake is cooked, remove from pan. Sprinkle sugar on pancake. Squeeze lime juice over sugar. Roll or fold pancake and serve.

BATTER

Savoury Vegetarian Pancake (Kuih Dadar Pedas – Hidangan Vegetarian)

For Batter

120 g/4 oz/4 tbsp wheat flour (*tepung gandum*)
¼ tsp salt
1 egg
¼ grated coconut to get 280 ml/½ pt thin coconut milk

Ingredients to be Mixed with Batter

2 tbsp oil
1 tsp mustard seeds (*biji sawi*)
1 sprig curry leaves
6 shallots
1 green chilli
1 red chilli

Other Ingredients

2 screwpine leaves/*pandan* leaves – knotted
1 tbsp oil
chilli sauce

To Make Batter

- Follow basic recipe of Thin Batter Using Wheat Flour.

To Prepare Ingredients to be Mixed with Batter

- Wash and wipe dry mustard seeds and curry leaves.
- Shred finely curry leaves, green and red chillies.
- Slice shallots lengthwise.
- Heat oil, lower fire. Sauté curry leaves and mustard seeds till there is nice aroma.
- Turn off fire. Leave to cool.
- Add vegetables and fried mixture to batter. Mix well.

To Make Vegetarian Pancake

- Heat pan lightly. Use knotted screwpine leaves to grease pan with a little oil.
- Stir batter mixture well. Use a ladle to pour enough batter into pan. Rotate pan to get a thin, round pancake. Do not over heat pan. Use low fire.
- When the under-side is golden brown, loosen the edges and turn over to cook the other side.
- When cooked, remove pancake onto a flat plate.
- Roll or fold pancake. Serve with chilli sauce. Refer to section on Sauces.

BATTER

Savoury Pancake Roll (Kuih Dadar Pedas)

For Batter
120 g/4 oz/4 tbsp wheat flour
(*tepung gandum*)
¼ tsp salt
1 egg
¼ grated coconut to get 280 ml/½ pt
thin coconut milk

For Filling
½ small yam bean/jicama (*sengkuang*)
½ small carrot
4 French beans
4 shallots
1 tbsp dried shrimps
⅛ tsp salt or to taste
⅛ tsp pepper
2 tbsp oil

Other Ingredients
2 screwpine leaves/*pandan* leaves
1 tbsp oil
chilli sauce

To Make Batter
- Follow basic recipe of Thin Batter Using Wheat Flour.

To Make Filling
- Soak dried shrimps.
- Slice finely shallots and French beans.
- Shred finely carrot and yam bean.
- Strain and chop dried shrimps finely.
- Heat oil. Sauté shallots till golden brown. Dish out.
- Sauté dried shrimps till you get nice aroma.
- Add vegetables, salt and pepper. Mix well.

- Add 1-2 tbsp water and simmer for a while until almost dry. Mix in fried shallots.

To Make Savoury Pancake Roll
- Follow instructions for Pancake with Grated Coconut Filling (*Kuih Ketayap*) in this section.
- Serve savoury pancake rolls with chilli sauce. Refer to section on Sauces.

N.B. You may use milk as liquid in the batter in place of thin coconut milk.

Suggested Savoury Fillings
* Sardin Filling – Refer to recipe of Sardine Rolls in Pastry Section.
* Dry Curry Meat Filling – Refer to recipe of Curry Puffs in Pastry Section.
* Dried Shrimp *Sambal* Filling – Refer to recipe of Dried Shrimp *Sambal* in section on Fish.
* Anchovy *Sambal* – Refer to recipe of Anchovy *Sambal* (*Sambal Ikan Bilis*) in section on Fish.
* Meat *Rendang* Filling – Refer to recipe of Meat *Rendang*/Spicy Meat in Coconut Milk (*Rendang Daging*) in section on Meat.

BATTER

Pancake with Grated Coconut Filling
(Kuih Ketayap)

For Batter
120 g/4 g/4 tbsp wheat flour (*tepung gandum*)

¼ tsp salt

1 egg

¼ grated coconut to get 280 ml/½ pt thin coconut milk

4 *pandan* leaves to get 1 - 2 tbsp thick *pandan* juice or

¼ tsp *pandan* essence

a few drops of green colouring

For Filling
½ grated white coconut

3 dsp palm sugar (*gula melaka*)

3 dsp sugar

3 dsp water

¼ tsp salt

2 screwpine leaves/*pandan* leaves – knotted

Other Ingredients
2 screwpine leaves/*pandan* leaves – knotted

1 tbsp oil

To Make Batter
- Follow basic recipe of Thin Batter Using Wheat Flour.
- Add *pandan* juice or *pandan* essence and colouring together with the second quantity of liquid.

To Make Coconut Filling
- Follow recipe of Steamed Glutinous Rice with Grated Coconut Topping (*Pulut Inti*) section on Local Kuih.

To Make Pancake with Grated Coconut Filling
- Heat pan lightly. Use knotted screwpine leaves to grease pan with a little oil.
- Stir batter well.
- Use a ladle to pour enough batter onto pan. Rotate pan to get a thin round pancake. Do not over heat pan. Use low fire.
- When the under-side is golden brown, loosen the edges and turn over to cook the other side.
- When cooked, remove pancake onto a flat plate.
- Spoon enough coconut filling onto pancake. Fold sides and make into a roll. Refer to photographs and instructions given. Serve.

N.B. You may use milk and yellow or green colouring in place of thin coconut milk.

BATTER

(i)   Shape the filling into a rectangle.

(ii)   Fold up bottom edge to cover filling.

(iii) Fold the two sides.

(iv) Make into a roll.

BATTER

Baked Coconut Milk Cake
(Kuih Bakar)

For Batter

120 g/4 oz/4 tbsp wheat flour (*tepung gandum*)
¼ tsp salt
2 eggs
2 - 3 tbsp sugar or to taste
½ grated coconut to get 280 ml/½ pt coconut milk
¼ tsp *pandan* essence
green or yellow colouring

Utensil

Kuih bakar mould or a pyrex dish

- Sift together flour and salt into a mixing bowl.
- Mix in sugar.
- Make a well in the centre. Break in eggs and add in ½ coconut milk.

- Mix to a smooth consistency. Do not allow the mixture to be doughy or lumpy.
- If batter is too thick, add more coconut milk, a little at a time.
- When the mixture is smooth, beat the batter for a few minutes until bubbles appear on the surface.
- Add in remaining coconut milk, essence and colouring. Mix well. Allow the batter to stand for 20 - 30 minutes.
- Stir batter thoroughly. Pour batter into greased *kuih bakar* mould or pyrex dish and bake in preheated oven 190°C/375°F /5 for 20 - 30 minutes until cooked.
- Remove cake from oven.
- Cool cake before cutting into suitable sizes. Serve.

Variation

* You may steam the batter instead of baking.

BATTER

Dried Shrimps In Fried Batter
(Cucur Udang/Cucur Bawang)

For Batter

60 g/2 oz/2 tbsp wheat flour (*tepung gandum*)

a pinch of salt or to taste

½ tsp curry powder – optional

1 egg

70 ml/⅛ pt water

Ingredients to be Mixed With Batter

1 tbsp dried shrimps (*udang kering*)

1 red chilli

1 green chilli

1 stalk spring onion

3 shallots

Other Ingredients

1 large bowl oil

To Make Batter

- Sift wheat flour, salt and curry powder (if used) into a mixing bowl. Make a well in the centre.
- Break in egg and add water.
- Beat till smooth. Allow to stand for 20 - 30 minutes.

To Prepare Other Ingredients

- Soak, strain and chop dried shrimps finely.
- Slice shallots lengthwise finely.
- Slice chillies finely. Chop spring onion finely.

To Make Dried Shrimps in Fried Batter

- Add all the prepared ingredients into the batter. Mix well.
- Drop the mixture with a spoon into the heated oil to deep fry till golden brown.
- Drain well and serve with chilli sauce. Refer to section on Sauces.

Variation

* Use 90 g/3 oz small prawns in place of dried shrimps.

BATTER

Sweet Half Egg-shaped Cake (Kuih Cara Manis)

For Batter
120 g/4 oz/4 tbsp wheat flour (*tepung gandum*)
¼ tsp salt
1 egg
½ grated coconut to get 280 ml/½ pt thin coconut milk
1 tbsp pandan juice/¼ tsp *pandan* essence
a few drops of green or yellow colouring

For Filling
1 tsp chopped palm sugar (*gula melaka*)
1 tsp sugar } mix together

Other Ingredients
1 tbsp oil
1 screwpine leaf/*pandan* leaf – knotted

Utensil
patitin or *Kuih Cara* mould

To Make Batter
- Follow basic recipe of Thin Batter Using Wheat Flour in this section.
- Add *pandan* juice or *pandan* essence and colouring together with second quantity of liquid.

To Cook Sweet Half Egg-shaped Cake
- Heat mould lightly. Use knotted screw-pine leaf to grease mould.
- Stir batter thoroughly. Use a spoon to pour in enough batter to fill half of the mould.
- Add ½ tsp filling.
- Cover filling with batter. Cover the moulds and cook *kuih cara* cake over fire for 5 -10 minutes.
- If patitin is used, bake in preheated oven 375°F/190°C/5 for 10 - 15 minutes.
- When cooked, remove cover. Leave for a short while. Loosen sides of cake and remove from moulds.

Suggested Sweet Filling
* Grated Coconut Filling – Refer to recipe of Steamed Glutinous Rice with Grated Coconut Topping (*Pulut Inti*) in Local Kuih section.
* Pineapple Jam Filling – Refer to recipe of Pineapple Jam Tarts in Pastry section.

Suggested Savoury Filling
* Dried Shrimp *Sambal*– Refer to section on Fish.
* Dry Curry Meat Filling – Refer to recipe of Curry Puffs in Pastry section.

BATTER

Savoury Pancake Net (Roti Jala)

For Batter

120 g/4 oz/4 tbsp wheat flour (*tepung gandum*)

¼ tsp salt

1 egg

¼ grated coconut to get 280 ml/½ pt thin coconut milk

yellow colouring – optional

Other Ingredients

2 screwpine leaves/*pandan* leaves – knotted

1 tbsp oil

Utensil

roti jala mould or perforated ladle

To Prepare Batter

- Follow basic recipe of Thin Batter Using Wheat Flour.
- Add colouring, if used, together with second quantity of liquid.

To Make *Roti Jala*

- Heat pan lightly. Use knotted screwpine leaves to grease pan with a little oil.
- Stir batter well.
- Pour enough batter through a perforated ladle or *roti jala* mould.
- Swirl the ladle or mould in a cirle to form a thin round net. Do not over heat pan. Use low fire.
- When batter is cooked and under-side is golden brown, remove to a flat plate.

Suggestions for Serving

* Make into a roll or fold into quarters. Serve separately with one of the following dish:

(a) Meat curry – Refer to section on Meat.

(b) Meat *rendang*/Spicy Meat in Coconut Milk (*Rendang Daging*) – Refer to section on Meat.

(c) Anchovy sambal with *belimbing* fruits (*sambal ikan bilis dengan buah belimbing besi*) – Refer to section on Fish.

* Wrap up filling with the pancake net by following methods in the recipe of Pancake with Grated Coconut Filling (*Kuih Ketayap*) in this section. You may choose one of the following fillings.

(a) Anchovy *sambal* (*Sambal ikan bilis*) – Refer to section on Fish.

(b) Dried shrimp *sambal* – Refer to section on Fish.

(c) Meat *Rendang*/Spicy Meat in Coconut Milk (*Rendang Daging*) – Refer to section on Meat.

(d) Fried spicy meat (*Daging Goreng Berempah*) – Refer to section on Meat.

(e) Dry curry meat – Refer to filling for curry puffs, section on Pastry.

BATTER

Banana Drop Scone/Banana Girdle Scone

For Batter
120 g/4 oz/4 tbsp wheat flour (*tepung gandum*)
1 tsp baking powder
or [¼ tsp soda bicarbonate
½ tsp cream of tartar]
¼ tsp salt
1 tbsp sugar
4 tbsp milk
1 egg

Other Ingredients
1 tbsp margarine/butter
1 or 2 cooking bananas

- Sift together wheat flour, salt and baking powder or soda bicarbonate and cream of tartar in a mixing bowl.
- Mix in sugar.
- Make a well in the centre.
- Break in egg. Add milk. Mix and beat to a smooth, thick consistency.
- Add lightly mashed banana. Mix well.
- Heat a frying pan or hot plate. Use a crushed grease proof paper to grease pan with a little margarine.
- Stir batter well.
- Use a spoon to pour enough batter onto pan to form a small round piece of about 5 cm/2" in diameter. Do not over heat pan. Use low fire.
- When the under-side is golden brown, turn over to cook the other side.

- When cooked, remove from pan. Serve.
- Several pieces can be cooked together at the same time.

Variation
* Mashed papaya can be added in place of mashed bananas.

Thin Batter Using Dry Rice Flour – Basic Recipe

120 g/4 oz/4 tbsp dry rice flour (*tepung beras*)
¼ tsp salt
enough liquid to get 560 ml/1 pt ready batter
¼ tsp alkali water

- Sift together rice flour and salt into a mixing bowl.
- Make a well in the centre and pour in 280 ml/½ pt liquid. Mix well. If batter is too thick add more liquid.
- Beat mixture till smooth. Strain mixture into a measuring jug.
- Pour in enough liquid to get 560 ml/1 pt batter.
- Allow to stand for 20 - 30 minutes.
- Just before use, add alkali water and stir thoroughly.

N.B. Syrup and coconut milk can be used as liquid for batter.

BATTER

Palm Sugar Batter Cake (Kuih Kosui)

For Batter

120 g/4 oz/4 tbsp dry rice flour (*tepung beras*)

¼ tsp salt

2 tbsp chopped palm sugar (*gula melaka*)

2 tbsp sugar

140 ml/¼ pt water

2 screwpine leaves/*pandan* leaves – knotted

} syrup to be used as liquid

For Coating Batter Cake

½ grated white coconut mixed with
¼ tsp salt or
desiccated coconut without salt

Utensil

Steaming tray 15 cm/6" in diameter and
5 cm/2" high or pyrex dish

To Make Syrup

- Boil together palm sugar, water and screwpine leaves.
- Stir to dissolve sugar.
- Remove screwpine leaves. Cool syrup.

To Make Batter

- Follow basic recipe of Thin Batter Using Rice Flour.
- If quantity of syrup is not enough, add water to make up 560 ml/1 pt batter.

To Cook Palm Sugar Batter Cake

- Heat steaming tray in the steamer.
- Add alkali water to batter and stir thoroughly.
- Without removing steaming tray from steamer, pour batter into a heated tray. Steam for 20 - 30 minutes using low fire.
- When batter is cooked remove from the tray. Cool batter thoroughly before cutting into suitable sizes.
- Toss in grated coconut and serve.

N.B. Avoid condensed water from steamer cover falling on to surface of batter by covering tray with grease proof paper or wiping steamer cover occasionally.

BATTER

Steamed Small Cup Rice Cake
(Kuih Lompang)

For Batter

120 g/4 oz/4 tbsp dry rice flour (*tepung beras*)
¼ tsp salt
4 tbsp sugar
140 ml/¼ pt water
2 screwpine leaves/*pandan* leaves
– knotted
colouring as desired
¼ tsp alkali water

} syrup to be used as liquid

For Cake Topping

2 tbsp grated white coconut mixed with
¼ tsp salt or
desiccated coconut without salt

Utensil

small Chinese wine cups/*kuih lompang* moulds

To Make Syrup

- Boil sugar with water and screwpine leaves.
- Stir till sugar dissolves.
- Remove screwpine leaves.
- Cool syrup.

To Make Batter

- Follow basic recipe of Thin Batter Using Dry Rice Flour in this section.
- If quantity of syrup is not enough, add water to make up the 560 ml/1 pt batter.

To Cook Rice Cake

- Place wine cups in a tray.
- Heat cups in steamer.

- Add alkali water to batter.
- Add a few drops of colouring to whole quantity of batter. Or you may also divide batter into desired portions and add a different colour to each portion.
- Stir thoroughly and spoon batter into cups.
- Steam batter for 10-15 minutes till cooked.
- Remove cups from tray. Cool cakes thoroughly before removing from cups.
- Spoon grated coconut on top of cake and serve.

Variation

* Use 2 tbsp chopped palm sugar (*gula melaka*) and 2 tbsp sugar for syrup but leave out colouring.

BATTER

Savoury Steamed Pudding
(Kuih Talam Berlauk)

For Batter

180 g/6 g/6 tbsp dry rice flour (*tepung beras*)

1 tsp curry powder

½ tsp salt

½ grated coconut to get 560 ml/1 pt coconut milk

½ tsp alkali water

Ingredients to be Mixed with Batter

150 g/5 oz prawns

½ tsp curry powder

½ tsp sugar

Ingredients for Garnishing
Savoury Steamed Pudding

1 egg

1 tbsp water

a pinch of salt

a pinch of pepper

} to make omelette

2 red chillies

1 stalk spring onion

4 shallots

3 tbsp oil

Utensil

a steaming tray 15 cm/6" in diameter and 5 cm/2" high

To Make Batter

- Sift together rice flour, 1 tsp curry powder and salt into a mixing bowl.
- Make a well in the centre of the dry ingredients.
- Pour in ½ amount of coconut milk and beat till smooth.

- Add in remaining coconut milk.
- Mix thoroughly. Allow batter to stand for 20 - 30 minutes.

To Prepare Other Ingredients

- Dice prawns. Season with ½ tsp curry powder and ½ tsp sugar.
- Slice finely spring onions, chillies and shallots.
- Make omelette and shred finely.
- Heat 3 tbsp oil. Fry shallots till golden brown over low fire. Dish out. Fry seasoned prawns for a few minutes. Dish out.

To Cook Savoury Pudding

- Heat steaming tray in steamer.
- Add alkali water to batter. Mix thoroughly.
- Add prawns and mix well.
- Without removing steaming tray from steamer, pour in batter.
- Steam batter for 20-30 minutes till cooked.
- Remove tray from steamer.
- Springkle mixture of omelette, chillies, spring onions and fried shallots on pudding.
- Press lightly to allow garnishes to settle on the pudding. Leave to cool before cutting pudding into suitable sizes.
- Serve with chilli sauce. Refer to section on Sauces.

Variation

* You may use 2 tbsp dried shrimps in place of prawns.

BATTER

Steamed Layered Pudding (Kuih Lapis)

For Batter

180 g/6 oz/6 tbsp dry rice flour (*tepung beras*)

¼ tsp salt

6 tbsp sugar ⎫

140 ml/¼ pt water ⎪ for syrup

4 screwpine leaves/*pandan* leaves ⎬ to be used as

– knotted ⎪ liquid

1 grated coconut to get 560 ml/1 pt ⎭

coconut milk

red colouring

¾ tsp alkali water

Utensil

a steaming tray 15 cm/6" in diameter and 5 cm/2" high

To Make Syrup

- Melt sugar in water with screwpine leaves. Stir to dissolve sugar.
- Remove screwpine leaves. Cool syrup.

To Make Batter

- Sift together rice flour and salt into a mixing bowl.
- Make a well in the centre. Add in syrup and 140 ml/¼ pt coconut milk.
- Beat mixture until smooth.
- Add in remaining coconut milk and mix thoroughly.
- Strain batter into a jug. Allow batter to stand for 20 - 30 minutes.
- Heat steaming tray in a steamer.
- Add alkali water to batter and mix well.
- Divide batter into two portions.
- Add a few drops of red colouring to one portion to get a pinkish batter.
- Divide each portion into three parts again.
- Without removing steaming tray from steamer pour one uncoloured part into tray. Steam it for three minutes till the thin layer of batter is set and almost cooked.
- Pour the pinkish part of the batter over the almost cooked uncoloured part and steam for three minutes till the batter is almost cooked.
- Repeat with the alternate layer of pinkish and uncoloured batter till the last part of the pinkish batter is left.
- Add a small drop of red colouring to the pinkish batter to get a layer of red batter for the top layer.
- When the top most layer which is red in colour is cooked, remove tray and cool thoroughly before cutting the pudding into suitable sizes.

N.B. Stir the batter thoroughly before pouring onto the last cooked layer. Avoid condensed water from falling onto surface of batter by wiping steamer cover every time after pouring in batter for the next layer.

BATTER

Steamed Green and White Layered Pudding (Kuih Talam)

For Batter to be Used as Bottom Layer of Pudding

120 g/4 oz/4 tbsp dry rice flour (*tepung beras*)

¼ tsp salt

5 tbsp sugar ⎫

140 ml/¼ pt water ⎬ to make syrup

2 screwpine leaves/*pandan* leaves – knotted ⎭

2 tbsp *pandan* juice

½ tsp *pandan* essence

a few drops of green colouring

½ tsp alkali water

For Batter to be Used as Top Layer of Pudding

90 g/3 oz/3 tbsp dry rice flour

¼ tsp salt

1 grated coconut to get 420 ml/¾ pt coconut milk

¼ tsp alkali water

Utensil

1 steaming tray 15 cm/6" in diameter and 5 cm/2" high

To Make Syrup

- Dissolve sugar in water with screwpine leaves over low fire.
- Stir till sugar dissolves. Remove screwpine leaves. Cool syrup.

To Make Batter for Bottom Layer

- Follow basic recipe of Thin Batter Using Dry Rice Flour.
- Add *pandan* juice or *pandan* essence and colouring.
- Pour batter into measuring jug.
- If quantity of syrup is not enough, add water to make up 560 ml/1 pt batter required.

To Cook Bottom Layer of Pudding

- Heat steaming tray in steamer.
- Add alkali water to batter and stir thoroughly.
- Without removing steaming tray from steamer, pour batter into heated tray.
- Steam for 20-30 minutes. Do not use high fire.

To Make Batter for Top Layer

- Sift together rice flour and salt into a mixing bowl.
- Put in half amount of coconut milk and beat mixture till smooth.
- Add the remaining coconut milk into the mixture. Mix well. Keep aside.

To Cook Top Layer of Pudding

- When bottom layer of batter is cooked, add in ¼ tsp alkali water to batter for top layer.
- Mix well.
- Slowly pour batter on top of bottom layer of cooked batter.
- Steam newly added batter for 15 - 20 minutes till cooked.
- Remove tray and cool thoroughly before cutting the pudding into suitable sizes. Serve.

Variation

* For bottom layer of batter, use 2½ tbsp chopped palm sugar (*gula melaka*) and 2½ tbsp sugar and leave out the green colouring.

N.B. Avoid condensed water from steamer falling onto surface of batter by wiping steamer cover every time it is lifted.

BATTER

Thick Batter Using Wheat Flour – Basic Recipe

The coating of food with this batter is crispy when hot but becomes soft when cold.

60 g/2 oz/2 tbsp wheat flour (*tepung gandum*)
a pinch of salt
1 egg
70 ml/⅛ pt water

- Sift wheat flour and salt into a bowl.
- Make a well in the centre.
- Break in egg and add water.
- Beat egg till smooth and allow to stand for 10 - 15 minutes before using.

Thick Batter Using Dry Rice Flour – Basic Recipe

The coating of food with this batter is crispier but the texture becomes hard when cold.

2 tbsp dry rice flour (*tepung beras*)
a pinch of salt
4 - 6 tbsp water
⅛ tsp slake lime (*kapur*)

- Sift rice flour and salt into a bowl.
- Make a well in the centre.
- Pour in 4 tbsp water and mix to a smooth batter. Add more water if required.
- Allow batter to stand for 10 - 15 minutes.
- Mix in slake lime just before use.

Thick Batter Using A Mixture of Flour – Basic Recipe

The coating of batter with a thick batter of mixture of flour is crispy when hot and is not hard when cold.

1 dsp rice flour
1 dsp cornflour (*tepung jagung*)
1 dsp wheat flour (*tepung gandum*)
a pinch of salt
4 - 6 tbsp water
⅛ tsp slake lime (*kapur*)

- Sift the flour and salt into a bowl.
- Make a well in the centre.
- Pour in 4 tbsp water. Mix to a thick smooth batter.
- Add more water if required.
- Leave batter to stand for 10 - 15 minutes.
- Add slake lime just before use.

BATTER

Banana Fritters (Pisang Goreng)

4 cooking bananas *e.g. pisang raja*
thick coating batter (own choice)
1 large bowl oil

Make batter following method of thick batter chosen in this section.

- Cut bananas into halves lengthwise.
- Add slake lime to batter for batter which needs slake lime. Mix well.
- Dip bananas one piece at a time into batter.
- Slide coated bananas into heated oil. Deep fry till golden brown over low fire.
- Drain oil before serving.

Variations

* The following ingredients can be coated and fried.
  (a) 150 g/5 oz sweet potatoes of the yellow variety – sliced.
  (b) 150 g/5 oz yam/taro – sliced.

BATTER

Pineapple Fritters

½ pineapple

For Batter
60 g/2 oz/2 tbsp wheat flour (*tepung gandum*)
a pinch of salt
1 egg
70 ml/⅛ pt water or milk

Other Ingredients
1 large bowl oil

For Syrup
2 tbsp golden syrup
1 tsp hot water

- Mix the golden syrup with hot water.
- Pour golden syrup on pineapple fritters and serve.

To Make Batter
- Sift wheat flour and salt into a bowl.
- Make a well in the centre.
- Break in egg and add in liquid.
- Beat thoroughly to get a smooth batter.
- Allow batter to stand for 10 - 15 minutes.

To Make Pineapple Fritters
- Skin and remove eyes and core from pineapple.
- Slice pineapple crosswise 1½ cm/½" thick.
- Dip pineapple slices in batter.
- Slide coated pineapple into heated oil.
- Deep fry till golden brown. Drain oil.

Variations
* You may serve pineapple fritters with treacle or honey in place of golden syrup.
* Instead of pineapples use bananas for this recipe.

PASTRY

PASTRY

Short Crust Pastry – Basic Recipe

120 g/4 oz wheat flour (*tepung gandum*)
¼ tsp salt
60 g/2 oz frozen margarine
2 - 3 dsp ice water

- Sift flour and salt into a mixing bowl.
- Add fat to flour. Cut fat into small pieces in the flour.
- Lift the flour to incorporate air by using finger tips.
- Rub fat into flour until mixture resembles bread crumbs. Do not over rub the fat because it will melt.
- Mix enough ice water into the flour until the mixture holds together.
- Use finger tips to draw the dough together till it leaves the sides of the bowl clean. The amount of water used depends on the dryness of the flour.

- Knead dough lightly on a pastry board that has been sprinkled with a little flour to prevent it from sticking to board.
- Roll out pastry evenly using short, light movements. Do not turn pastry over.
- Roll to 3 mm/⅛" thick for pastry to be baked and a little thinner for pastry to be fried.
- Do not pull or stretch pastry. Cut into rounds or other shapes and use as required.
- Put to bake in a preheated oven 200°C/400°F/6 for 10 - 15 minutes or deep fry.

N.B. To avoid drying pastry, roll out half of the portion first and cover the other half with a damp cloth.

Variation
* You may use 30 g/1 oz margarine and 30 g/1 oz butter instead of using all margarine.

PASTRY

Peanut Puffs

For Pastry
120 g/4 oz wheat flour (*tepung gandum*)
¼ tsp salt
60 g/2 oz frozen margarine
2 - 3 dsp ice water

For Filling
3 tbsp peanuts
1 tbsp sesame seeds
1 tbsp castor sugar

Other Ingredient
1 large bowl oil for deep fat frying

To Make Filling
- Fry sesame seeds without oil over low fire till golden brown.
- Heat pan again. Fry peanuts without oil over low fire until peanut skins can be removed easily.
- Remove skins from peanuts.
- Chop or pound peanuts finely.
- Mix peanuts with sesame seeds and sugar.

To Make Pastry
- Follow basic recipe in this section.

To Make Peanut Puffs
- Follow instructions for making Curry Puffs in this section.
- Deep fry or bake the puffs.

Grated Coconut Puffs
(Kuih Sepang)

For Pastry
120 g/4 oz wheat flour (*tepung gandum*)
¼ tsp salt
60 g/2 oz frozen margarine
2 - 3 dsp ice water

For Filling
¼ grated coconut
3 dsp chopped palm sugar (*gula melaka*)
3 dsp sugar
3 dsp water
2 screwpine leaves/*pandan* leaves – knotted

Other Ingredient
1 large bowl oil for deep fat frying

To Make Filling
- Boil sugar with water till sugar dissolves.
- Add grated coconut and knotted screwpine leaves.
- Stir mixture till grated coconut has absorbed syrup and mixture is moist.
- Remove screwpine leaves.

To Make Pastry
- Follow basic recipe in this section.

To Make Grated Coconut Puffs
- Follow instructions for making Curry Puffs in this section in page 176 and 177.
- Deep fry or bake the puffs.

PASTRY

Curry Puffs

For Pastry

120 g/4 oz wheat flour (*tepung gandum*)
¼ tsp salt
60 g/2 oz frozen margarine
2 - 3 dsp ice water

For Dry Curry Meat Filling

90 g/3 oz minced meat
1 potato
1 onion
2 shallots
1 sprig curry leaves
1 tbsp curry powder
70 ml/⅛ pt water or coconut milk
½ tsp salt or to taste
2 tbsp oil

Other Ingredient

1 large bowl oil for deep fat frying

To Make Filling

- Dice potato finely. Soak in water.
- Dice onion finely.
- Slice shallots.
- Shred curry leaves finely.
- Blend curry powder into a paste with 1 - 2 tbsp water or coconut milk.
- Heat oil. Sauté shallots. Add curry leaves. Fry till there is nice aroma. Add curry paste. Fry till there is nice aroma and oil appears.
- Add meat. Fry for a minute. Add onion. Again fry for a minute.
- Add diced potatoes and salt. Mix well.
- Add remaining water or coconut milk and simmer till meat and vegetables are cooked and mixture is moist.
- Taste. Dish out to cool.

To Make Pastry

- Follow basic recipe in this section.

To Make Curry Puffs

- Roll out and cut pastry into rounds.
- Follow photographs and instructions given.
- Cover rounds of pastry with a damp cloth.
- Spoon filling into each round of pastry.
- Wet the edges with a little water.
- Fold over to cover filling.
- Seal the edges by twisting the edges or by pressing the edges together with a fork.
- Heat oil. Slide the curry puffs into the oil and deep fry till golden brown. Do not allow the oil to be smoking hot.

Variations in Cooking Method and Ingredient

* You may bake the curry puffs instead of deep frying them.
* You may use 90 g/3 oz small prawns in place of meat.

PASTRY

(i)   *Place pastry cutter on a rolled out pastry. Cut rounds of pastry.*

(ii)   *Spoon enough filling on half of the semi circle but do not spread too near to edge of pastry.*

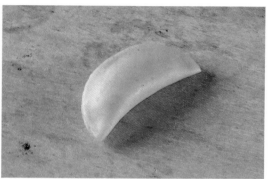

(iii)   *Wet edge of pastry. Cover the filling with the other semi circle of pastry. Press edges together to seal tightly.*

(iv)   *Decorate edge by pinching or twisting the edge or use a fork to press lines on the edge of pastry.*

PASTRY

Vegetable Puffs
(Epok-epok Sayur)

For Pastry

120 g/4 oz wheat flour (*tepung gandum*)
¼ tsp salt
60 g/2 oz frozen margarine
2 - 3 dsp ice water

For Filling

90 g/3 oz small prawns
½ tsp sugar
¼ tsp pepper
½ yam bean/jicama (*sengkuang*)
½ carrot
4 French beans
2 pips garlic
½ tsp salt
2 tbsp oil

Other Ingredient

1 large bowl oil for deep fat frying

To Make Filling

- Dice prawns. Season prawns with sugar and pepper.
- Shred finely yam bean, carrot and French beans.
- Chop garlic finely.
- Heat oil. Sauté garlic till golden brown.
- Add prawns. Fry for a short while.
- Add all the vegetables and salt. Mix well.
- Add 2 tbsp water. Allow mixture to simmer till vegetables are soft and mixture is moist.
- Dish out and cool.

To Make Pastry

- Follow basic recipe in this section.

To Make Vegetable Puffs

- Follow instructions for making Curry Puffs in this section.
- Deep fry or bake the puffs.
- Serve vegetable puffs with chilli sauce if desired. Refer to section on Sauces.

PASTRY

Spicy Savoury Puffs (Sepera)

For Pastry

120 g/4 oz wheat flour (*tepung gandum*)
¼ tsp salt
60 g/2 oz frozen margarine
2 - 3 dsp ice water

For Filling

¼ grated white coconut
2 dried chillies
1 tsp fennel (*jintan manis*)
1½ cm/½" cube dry turmeric
(*kunyit kering*)
1 tbsp dried shrimps (*udang kering*)
4 shallots
2 slices ginger
1 red chilli
1 stick lemon grass (*serai*)
½ tsp salt or to taste
2 tbsp oil

Other Ingredient

1 large bowl oil for deep fat frying

To Make Filling

- Wash and strain dried shrimps.
- Finely slice lemon grass. Slice shallots lengthwise finely.
- Dice finely ginger and red chilli.
- Heat pan/wok. Fry dried chillies, dry turmeric and fennel without oil over low fire. Do not wet the ingredients.
- Immediately use a dry pounder to pound the mixture into a fine powder. Spoon out.
- Pound dried shrimps.
- Heat oil. Lower fire. Fry chilli powder mixture until there is nice aroma. Add dried shrimps and fry till there is nice aroma. Add into mixture grated coconut, shallots, ginger, red chilli, lemon grass and salt. Mix well. Taste.

To Make Pastry

- Follow basic recipe in this section.

To Make Spicy Savoury Puffs

- Follow instructions for making Curry Puffs in this section.
- Deep fry or bake the puffs.

PASTRY

Vegetarian Puffs

For Pastry
120 g/4 oz wheat flour (*tepung gandum*)
¼ tsp salt
60 g/2 oz frozen margarine
2 - 3 dsp ice water

For Filling
1 potato
1 onion
½ carrot
2 shallots
1 slice ginger
1 sprig curry leaf
1 tsp mustard seeds (*biji sawi*)
1 tbsp curry powder or to taste
70 ml/⅛ pt water or coconut milk
½ tsp salt
2 tbsp oil

Other Ingredient
1 large bowl oil for deep fat frying

To Make Filling

- Wash and wipe dry curry leaves and mustard seeds.
- Shred curry leaves finely.
- Slice shallots finely.
- Dice potato finely and soak in water.
- Dice finely ginger, carrot and onion.
- Blend curry powder to a paste with 1 - 2 tbsp water or coconut milk.
- Heat oil. Lower fire. Sauté shallots till there is nice aroma. Add curry leaves, mustard seeds and ginger. Fry till there is nice aroma.
- Add curry powder paste. Fry till there is nice aroma and oil appears.
- Add in drained potato, onion, carrot and salt. Fry for a short while.
- Add remaining water or coconut milk. Simmer till vegetables are cooked and moist. Taste.
- Dish out to cool.

To Make Pastry

- Follow basic recipe in this section.

To Make Vegetarian Puffs

- Prepare a piece of grease proof paper 7½ cm/3" square.
- After rolling out pastry, use the square piece of grease proof paper as a guide to cut out square pieces of pastry.
- Cover square pieces of pastry with a damp cloth.
- Follow photographs and instructions given to make triangular vegetarian puffs.
- Deep fry or bake vegetarian puffs.

PASTRY

(i)   Place square grease proof paper on rolled out pastry. Cut out pastry with a palette knife.

(ii)   Spoon enough filling on one half of the triangle section.

(iii)   Wet the two edges. Enclose the filling with the other half of the triangle and seal the edges tightly.

(iv)   Use a fork to press lines at the edge of the pastry to form a pattern.

PASTRY

Dried Shrimp Sambal Puffs
(Paf Sambal Udang Kering)

For Pastry

120 g/4 oz wheat flour (*tepung gandum*)
¼ tsp salt
60 g/2 oz frozen margarine
2 - 3 dsp ice water

For Dried Shrimp *Sambal* Filling

2 tbsp dried shrimps (*udang kering*)
4 shallots
1 stick lemon grass (*serai*)
3 - 5 dried chillies
1½ cm/½" cube shrimp paste (*belacan*)
1 tsp tamarind paste (*asam jawa*)
2 tbsp water
¼ tsp salt ⎫
½ tsp sugar ⎬ or to taste
2 tbsp oil ⎭

- Soak dried chillies and dried shrimps separately. Strain.
- Slice lemon grass.
- Mix tamarind paste with water and strain.
- Pound dried shrimps and keep aside.
- Pound finely dried chillies, lemon grass, shallots and shrimp paste.
- Fry chilli mixture till there is nice aroma and oil appears.
- Add in dried shrimps. Fry lightly.
- Add in tamarind juice, sugar and salt.
- Mix well. Simmer till moist, stirring all the time and over low fire.

To Make Pastry

- Follow basic recipe in this section.

To Make Dried Shrimp *Sambal* Puffs

- Prepare a piece of grease proof paper 7½ cm/3" square.
- After rolling out pastry, use the square piece of grease proof paper as a guide to cut out square pieces of pastry.
- Cover square pieces of pastry with a damp cloth.
- Follow instructions and photographs given to make rectangular dried shrimp *sambal* puffs.
- Deep fry or bake the puffs.

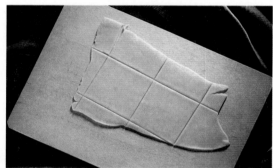

(i)   Place square grease proof paper on rolled out pastry and cut out pastry with a palette knife.

(ii)   Spoon enough filling onto half side of pastry.

PASTRY

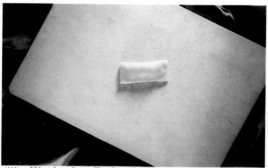

(iii) Wet the edges. Enclose the filling with the other half of pastry and seal the edges together tightly.

(iv) Use a fork to press lines at the edges of the pastry to form a pattern.

PASTRY

Sardine Rolls

For Pastry
120 g/4 oz wheat flour (*tepung gandum*)
¼ tsp salt
60 g/2 oz frozen margarine
2 - 3 dsp ice water

For Sardine Filling
2 sardines
enough sardine sauce to give a
moist texture
1 red chilli
½ onion
¼ tsp pepper
⅛ tsp salt   } or to
1 tsp lime juice   } taste

Other Ingredient
1 beaten egg for glazing

To Make Filling
- Remove bones from sardine. Mash sardines.
- Dice onion and chilli finely.
- Mix together all the ingredients and add enough sardine sauce to make a moist filling. Taste.

To Make Pastry
- Follow basic recipe in this section.

To Make Sardine Roll
- Prepare a piece of grease proof paper 5 × 7½ cm/2 × 3" rectangle.
- After rolling out pastry, use the rectangular piece of grease proof paper as a guide to cut out rectangular pieces of pastry.
- Cover pieces of pastry with a damp cloth.
- Follow intructions and photographs shown to make sardine rolls.
- Bake the sardine rolls in a preheated oven of 200°C/400°F/6 for 10 - 15 minutes.

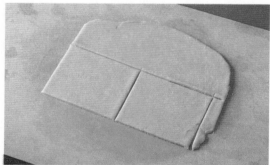

(i) Place rectangular piece of grease proof paper on rolled out pastry and cut out pastry with a palette knife.

(ii) Spoon enough filling and place along short side of pastry but do not reach too near the edges.

PASTRY

(iii) *Wet the other edges of the pastry. Roll the pastry over filling and press the wet edge to stick roll together.*

(iv) *Place rolls on baking tray. Use a fork to prick lines on the rolls. Brush top surface of rolls with beaten egg and bake.*

PASTRY

Pineapple Jam Tarts

For Pastry

120 g/4 oz wheat flour (*tepung gandum*)
¼ tsp salt
60 g/2 oz frozen margarine
2 - 3 dsp ice water

For Pineapple Jam Filling

1 pineapple
4 - 6 tbsp sugar or to taste
2½ cm/1" length cinnamon (*kayu manis*)
2 cloves (*bunga cengkih*)

To Make Pineapple Jam

- Skin and remove pineapple eyes. Grate pineapple.
- Strain juice but do not squeeze out juice until the grated pineapple is pulpy and dry.
- Put grated pineapple, sugar, cinnamon and cloves into a pot and bring to boil.
- Lower fire. Simmer till jam is thick and moist. Stir occassionally to prevent jam from sticking to pot and from being burnt.
- When jam is ready, it should not spread when a very small amount is dropped into cold water.

To Make Pastry

- Follow basic recipe in this section.

To Make Pineapple Jam Tarts

- Roll out pastry. Cut pastry into rounds with a fluted cutter.
- Line patitins with the round pieces of pastry. Press lightly into shape.
- Use a fork to prick the base of the pastry.
- Spoon pineapple jam onto each pastry.
- Use strips of pastry to form patterns on top of jam.

- Bake the tarts in a preheated oven of 200ºC/400ºF/6 for 15 - 20 minutes until pastry is cooked.

Variation

* You may place circular pieces of pastry on baking tray instead of using patitins. Spoon jam onto centre of the rounds of pastry and decorate with strips of pastry.

Suggestion

* Use the pineapple juice to make pineapple drink. Refer to section on Drinks.

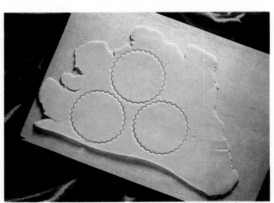

(i)   Use a fluted cutter to cut out circular pieces of pastry.

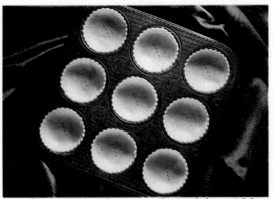

(ii) Line patitins with pastry and use a fork to prick base of pastry.

(iii) Spoon jam onto pastry.

(iv) Place strips of pastry to make decoration on jam.

PASTRY

Coconut Tarts

For Pastry
120 g/4 oz wheat flour (*tepung gandum*)
¼ tsp salt
60 g/2 oz frozen margarine
2 - 3 dsp ice water

For Filling
½ grated white coconut or
desiccated coconut
45 g/1½ oz margarine/butter
45 g/1½ oz castor sugar
1 - 2 tsp wheat flour (*tepung gandum*)
¼ tsp vanilla essence
½ egg

To Make Filling

- Cream fat and sugar until light and fluffy.
- Add in beaten egg and vanilla essence gradually. Beat well.
- Sift the flour into the creamed mixture to get a soft dropping consistency.
- Fold in grated coconut or enough desiccated coconut as desired.

To Make Pastry

- Follow basic recipe in this section.

To Make Coconut Tarts

- Follow instructions for making Pineapple Jam Tarts.
- Bake in a preheated oven of 200°C/ 400°F/6 for 15 - 20 minutes until pastry is cooked.

INDEX

INDEX

INDEX

INDEX

INDEX

Note

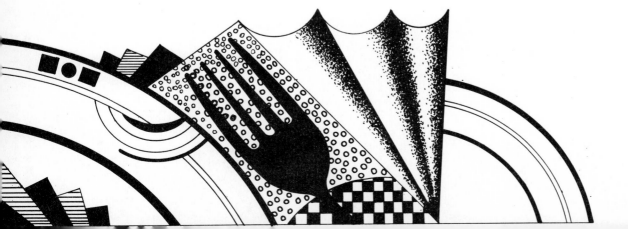